FROM REVELATIONS VOLUME III: PRISONER OF THE NEW JIM CROW

Sefu Thabiti Fatiu
Prechelle S. Shannon

ISBN-9798585013607

Cover design by: Copyright Owner
Library of Congress Control Number: PRE18979005091
Printed in the United States of America

To the Fallen but never Forgotten...

Table of Contents

Introduction

April 18, 2019

I was introduced to Michelle Alexander's historical work, "The New Jim Crow," in (2011) by a like-minded brotha' who was just a few short months away from making his transition to a minimum-security prison. At the time, I had been almost one year into my most recent transfer from one plantation to another place where I already put in time (10) years prior. At that point, I had almost (16) years in on my sentence and had done time in (6) prisons. I had been in every prison region in the state of Maryland, all medium to medium/maximum-security jails, wherein I've served a minimum of (2) years. To this date, I've been in (7) jails in (23+) years, served a maximum of (6) years on one plantation, and have been transferred a total of (9) times.

Inasmuch as I don't relish the idea of being shipped from one plantation to another, I made my peace with the conceptual fact that there is a distinct and well-defined difference between the plantation owner and those who tend to the slaves, in that the plantation owner only sees the bottom line of what the slave is worth in capital, while the attendant has to manage the discontent and temperament of the slave and the plantation as a whole. He has to see the slave as he stifles his dignity, struggling with his innate sense of self-worth and pride. He has to see the slave as he heals from the constant brutality used as a control mechanism to strip him of his will to live and erode his already fragile dexterity, and when the determination of the attendant wears in the face of the slave's utter insistence on decency and humanitarianism, it is then that the decision is made to cut all losses and ship the slave off to a different plantation. The same can be said when one becomes aware of their captive state in a state of captivity. Consciousness is the antithesis of enslavement, and day after day, it reigns true that there is no room for a conscious slave on any plantation. So, it follows that becoming conscious is not a tolerable endeavor in the eyes of the oppressor. In fact, becoming conscious is a declaration of war.

I was introduced to myself and awakened to my state of being within a few months into this incarceration. I met men who I came to admire because, on the surface, they displayed the qualities I'd always wanted to incorporate into my character but didn't know how. These men talked with intelligence; they spoke on principles, ideas...They spoke the language of logic and philosophized *the meaning of it all*. They were thoughtful and asked questions that provoked critical thinking. They gave me a seat at their bountiful and benevolent table. My only job, the one task I had, was to maintain that seat. I constantly found myself in absolute awe of these profound vessels of truth and wisdom; some of it, of course, was what we called *swift wisdom*, but it was wisdom, nonetheless. It was powerful and attractive. To be amongst these street philosophers placed you in an exclusive circle, and the objective for me was to catch up, keep up, and ultimately pass the front runner(s). I saw these men as not just teachers; they were righteous without being self-righteous; they were diplomats, tacticians, strategists; they were *uncs'* and fatherly figures, big brothers, scholars. These distinguished gentlemen were some of the finest examples of manhood I've ever seen, and most of these good, strong, militant men of moral rectitude were *dope fiends*.

The social ladder, the food chain, so to speak, in prison, is unique in that it isn't predicated on material wealth like it is in the broader society at large. As a matter of fact, an individual in prison can be *ballin'* completely out of control, wealthy according to every socially accepted standard of materials, but don't have the respect of the men. In this world, he's poor, destitute, and may at some point become prey. On the other hand, an individual can have little to nothing in material wealth, but if he has the respect of the men, this world becomes his oyster. I realized early on in this bid that I had the respect of the men when one of them handed me the keys to the castle...a book...

    ...If you'll continue to bear with me, I'd like to explain a personal incongruity. I am an excellent reader. I can spell all of the words that I know, and because of the way I was raised, I was able to hone in on my ability to write, but I've hated reading throughout my life. My household discipline was that you be quiet, and you listen to what you're being told, so that's how I was taught to learn. However, as much as I didn't enjoy reading, what I hated more, was being left out of a conversation of substance simply because I wasn't informed. I wanted desperately to have the ability to chime in on discussions that were political, philosophical, scientific, or historical. So, I had to read the works of some of our renowned scholars such as Dr. Na'im Akbar, Anthony Browder, Dr. Amos Wilson, Tony Martin, Frantz Fanon, Dr. Frances Cress Welsing, Haki Madhubuti, Cheik Anta Diop, John Henrik Clarke, George G.M. James, Chancellor Williams, Dr. Cornell West, Dr. Iyanla Vanzant, Prof. Angela Davis, Assata Shakur, Elaine Brown, Dr. Bobby E. Wright, James Baldwin, Sam Greenlee, Jomo Kenyatta, Dr. Molefi K. Asante, Jawanza Kunjufu, Maulana Karenga, Steve Biko, Kwame Ture, Sun Tzu, Huey P. Newton, Bobby Seale, Ivan Van Sertima, George Jackson, and Michelle Alexander, to name a short few out of a list that could go on and on. I also must give an honorable mention to Merriam-Webster Incorporated. By no means is this list a slight to any of my teachers that weren't named here, but if I were to name everyone, that would be a page in and of itself. I think I made my point. If not, I'll explain it this way...From (2001) to (2006), I read one book per week, every week, as was the discipline subscribed to. Again, I hated reading, but even more so, I hated the idea of being ignorant, so sacrifices had to be made.

    No two opposing forces can coexist in the same place at the same time when both seek to achieve the same end. This is the nature of warfare, so between proper education with advanced comprehension versus illiteracy, ignorance, and misinformation, naturally, a conflict must ensue, and I'd have to choose a side.

For me, of course, the choice is simple, but how often do we give credence to the fact that war is not only a natural phenomenon, but it is being waged all the time on various fronts? Quite often, warfare ensues with silent weapons, and many of us are oblivious when the explosions occur. I've been trained my entire life to learn in the auditory, so I can hear the things most people don't. More often than not, people only voice what they want others to hear or what they think people want to hear, although more of what we need to hear too often goes unspoken. Remember this... not every war ends with a decisive victory...

...So here it is, the (13th) Amendment to the United States Constitution is a clause, a compromise to the emancipation of the slaves that justifies the further use of slavery as a punishment for one being convicted of a crime; Circa (1865). However, in (1948), the General Assembly of the United States proclaimed in Article (4) of the Universal Declaration of Human Rights that, "No one shall be held in slavery or servitude; slavery and the slave trade shall be prohibited in all their forms." It leaves one to wonder how the U.S. can conduct itself as though it is the moral and ethical standard to the world when it refuses to dismantle a system that maintains second class citizenship and a culture of dehumanization for the sake of monetary wealth. Such acts completely undermine global law, natural law, and the fronts of human integrity and interactivity. The moral leader of the world owns over (2) million slaves. The ethical standard bearer is the hub of the largest human trafficking ring in the world. How many of us (2) million-plus were abducted as a result of our youthful indiscretions, held for ransom, and shipped off from one plantation to the next, at the whims of an overseer who may have never even seen a person of color until they took a job in the Prison Industrial Complex.

I know my personal history. I know what I've done and where I've been. I would never attempt to rationalize or make any justification for the things I've done. All I can do is accept accountability and work towards repairing the damage I left in my wake. The thing is, I sold drugs. I've sold marijuana, cocaine, and heroin in my youth, my indiscretions. What I didn't know then was that I was working for the United States government. See, these are the subtleties, the nuances of the situation we call *the game*, that we don't notice, tend to ignore, in denial of, or don't believe, even when the information is exposed. No, I didn't purchase my product from the C.I.A., but the information is out there that the C.I.A. flooded cities across America with illegal narcotics. This documented history coincides with the U.S. being the world's leader in narcotics/drug distribution and sales. So then, it follows that every flat-footed, hand-to-hand, nickel-and-dime, *corner-shop kingpin* sold, pitched, and peddled for the government in the final analysis. The capital gain in addiction is astronomical. We're talking about prison and imprisonment, which means we're talking about slavery and enslavement, so if we determine at any point that addiction is fundamental to and is an inextricable part of the conversation, then we must understand that authentically, addiction is another form of imprisonment. Addiction is a psychosis that enslaves the mind, body, and soul. It is a cultural reality for a people already assimilated into a herd mentality who have been systematically ushered into degeneracy. Where we find ourselves in this day and time is merely a commentary on what happens when a society is built on an aggregation of social abnormalities. Furthermore, our collective condition and conditioning are systemic of the core values of those who have reaped the bounties from the debasement and exploitation of generations of human beings and promote that those people move on from it as if the chapter of our history has been resolved.

How can this actually be accomplished here, when racism, just like the Trans-Atlantic Slave Trade, continues to evolve. The Prison Industrial Complex is neo-slavery. Classism, materialism, sexism, and religiosity is this generation's racism; so, you can recognize that East Baltimore was once considered the Heroin capital of the east coast for decades and still accept the idea of the *newness* of an opioid epidemic that is grounded in the abuse and addiction one develops to prescription drugs, such as Percocet, OxyContin, Suboxone, etc... The fact is, pills and/or barbiturates have always been embraced by white America. Still, it seems to me that now, the pharmaceutical companies have unleashed a more potent version of legal dope that is strangling the old idea of the *dope game*, so much so that the potency of heroin pales in comparison to "Percs," "Oxy's" or "Bennies." One takes a drug to heal them from an ailment and then has to take another drug to heal themselves of the side effect ailment(s) caused by the initial drug. The epidemic is just another bit of the nuances of the *game* we don't comprehend. Meaning, it's deeper than the notion we tend to toss around that ... "it wasn't a problem until white people are just as bad off as we are." No, a larger part of it is that the color lines are so blurred that what used to be a black thing has seeped into those *good*, affluent white communities, so we're closer to figuring out that we inherited white folk problems as opposed to it being the other way around.

Please pay close attention as I say this... slavery is a human condition that has existed since time immemorial. Every people had their own form of servitude and rationale behind it. Chattel slavery is a concoction born out of an abominable, diseased, maniacal creature. Only one brand of folk has ever even attempted to enlist such tactics that at one point gave audience to the very idea that, out of all of God's creation, any people should for one single, solitary moment be considered sub-human; and, since such a thought could ever be perceived as true, that those who have defined the condition has inherited the burden of cultivating these godless beings into civilized life. The question I now ask is simply this: "If this is true, then when will these saviors of ours be released from this burden?" I guess if one must consider my current state of affairs, maybe it could be argued that I'm not civilized enough, or maybe even at all. Damn...

...I needed to pause for a moment because I needed to consider whether I have ever, then, or now, given any air of legitimacy to such ideas that could guarantee I'd be classified as an incorrigible savage. If so, is it safe to assume that I've been walking around in blackface? I could argue that any black man or black woman who embraces these ideas or concepts are subservient proponents of white supremacy. Let's look at this... if I call you a nigger or nigga affectionately like I love calling you that, do I call you that because I love you? To think that we are so entrenched in this chaos that we are split on the debate on using the *N-word*. This explains much more than we care to discuss, so let's delve just a little... I recently watched a reality show where this very debate was put to the forefront of the theme for that episode. In this, we see a person of another race and culture blasting on social media some choice expletives about their black co-workers' behavior(s), and in those rantings used the word nigga(s). The Blacks went into an uproar about this person using the word unaffectionately and shamed this person for not knowing the word's painful history. In their defense, the person said, basically, "I hear you all calling each other that all of the time, so I didn't think I did anything wrong." To argue even further, the response was, and I'm paraphrasing, "This is our word. We use it differently. When we say it, it doesn't mean the same thing as when you say it. We say it out of love." I see all of this, and of course, I'm upset and analytical because, for one, it is painfully obvious that none of them know the history of that word, especially the Blacks on the show; two, it is even more obvious that we've bought into the process. I'm not sure what hurts more, that we can project and protect our own confusion and ignorance so convincingly that we'll confuse the hell out of everyone else, get loud and irate about it and then lambaste them for their lack of empathy and compassion; or that, when we're made to see just how fucked up it looks when we try to justify and rationalize why we can so easily caress one another with the right hand while choking us to death with the left hand, we seek pity. You can't love me while hating me. You can't hug me while you're pushing me away; the act cancels each other out. So now we're taking ownership of the word nigger? I don't get it. I don't get how there can be, at any point in our history, a legitimate and sound notion that we can or ever should consider nigger a part of us, like it's who we are and how we identify with one another. It's sick logic. Just because we've used a term loosely doesn't change the word's definition, and to drive my point, no one else of a different ethnicity can utter the word without consequence. So, are we niggers? No. Have we and do we take on the attributes of niggers? Sure, we do. Especially when we compromise our collective and personal dignity because we would rather align ourselves with a trend that promotes self-hatred as a way of life. I can go on and on with this. Maybe the subject will be revisited later on. Still, for now, we have to do better or continue to suffer the consequences of our acceptance of falling short of even mediocracy intellectually, economically, politically, spiritually, psychologically, and culturally.

Have I ever, whether consciously or unconsciously, legitimized the stigmatism and stereotypes that were kicked around by politicians and the media alike to justify why and how I've found myself living inside of such dismal circumstances? I'm a member of the generation that was born in between the *Black Power Era* and *Reganomics*. When the government had definitively and decisively waged a strategic campaign to disrupt, corrupt, and ultimately destroy black unity, black power, and black love, I was in the womb. My life began in an age of defiance, and I grew up uncomfortable in my own skin but could never understand why. I questioned everything, silently, because to speak out was tantamount to being disrespectful, which had its own dreadful consequences. Periodically, I'd find myself unable to stifle my confusion, and before I knew it, my ass would find its way on the business end of a thick leather belt. I'd speak out on how Santa Claus couldn't possibly be real, 'cause none of the houses in the neighborhood had chimneys, so he can't get in. I was forced to believe, or at least surrender to the idea that Santa was undoubtedly real or suffer the full wrath of a reality where Santa is a lie. What would you do? I questioned the church. I questioned the schools, and because these doubts and my confusion had at many points throughout my childhood become so pervasive, I'd lose control and become enraged at being condescended to and patronized. I'm (5, 6, 7) years old, and I'm having fits because I'm struggling to understand and comprehend the logic and why's and how's the adults are being challenged to help me realize. They struggle with me, and I'm frustrated with them rationalizing my output is me being "slow," so finally, I explode. They say I'm throwing "temper tantrums." I obviously can't explain what just happened, so I have to prepare for the inevitable. I got my ass whipped so much that one time my father beat the shiny side from the leather belt. I was always punished and made to stay in the house for long periods ranging from several weeks to several months. To this very day, I try to imagine what I looked like in a world that was so alien to me because it seemed like people enjoyed living and perpetuating obvious contradictions. For this reason, I've always been able to be good in my own space, mentally and physically. In fact, I need that to process what I'm presented with mentally and physically, and it's because I've always had to figure it out on my own if I'm going to progress. So, in those times where I longed to go out and be amongst my peers, I lived in my head and had powerful dreams of an abstract reality full of quiet people who vibe with me to soulful rhythms and dramatic beats...

...By the time I was (13) years old, I had already experienced heartbreak and chastisement. I find myself now explaining to myself that my parents and elders, are the survivors of a vicious system of ultra-aggressive, invasive actions that rocked their world, so much so that they lost their minds. They were attacked daily, some of them killed, but most were forever crippled by the enemy, so many sought that abstract reality. Some of them got lost and never made it back. Meanwhile, the children were being taught the Pledge of Allegiance instead of the Black Child's Pledge. We were taught about George Washington instead of George Jackson. We learned about the Battle of Antietam instead of Attica. I suspect that many of the beatings I received at home were an attempt to save me from the disfiguring whippings I'd surely received from the Slavers if my discontent persisted. I tried to imagine that my mother realized that the spirit of the revolution was enriched in my DNA and so, much like the mothers on the old plantations, she tried in earnest to stymie my rebellious nature so that the Slavers wouldn't feel threatened by my existence and take me away from her or from here. Such attempts are to no avail if you can't change my perception of reality. So eventually, I, just like all of those (70's) babies, will wind up at the same crossroads, deciding to accept the version of reality you're taught, the version you're immersed in, or the reality you define.

My parents and elders are survivors of something that I was never taught existed. I was taught about Santa Claus and the Easter Bunny, but not about racism and the social caste that maintains poverty, promotes deviancy, and instigates violence. I was inculcated with stories about the miracles performed by Jesus but never forewarned of the atrocities committed in Jesus' good name. I got to see film footage, movies, and documentaries about Martin Luther King Jr., but as much as I love the good Dr. King, I needed just as much, if not more, information on the good Pastor Nat Turner. It's not a coincidence that the same Warden that insisted we watched the movie "Selma" stopped us from being able to watch "Birth of a Nation." My ancestors, elders, and my parents were beaten to a pulp, and just as the age of defiance began to give birth to a new, more resilient and determined progeny, Ronald Reagan assumed the helm where Richard Nixon's War On Drugs left off and stepped up all avaricious methods of debilitating an already injured community. He sold us cheap narcotics and drop-shipped cheap, obsolete guns. He built concentration camps and created a media circus around the crime and violence his enforcers and overseers initiated and instigated. He and his cohorts and successors targeted and labeled an entire generation born in captivity and raised in desolation. Little did I know, I was labeled scientifically by the leading criminologists of the day as a *Super Predator*. What is one to do?

None of what I said in the before mentioned passages are

to be taken as an excuse for anything I've ever done in my life, but if any of what I said has an atom's weight of truth in it, could it possibly explain my approach as I've made my attempts at addressing my reality? Or, is all I've said so far the very thing that legitimizes the fact that not only am I a slave of the Prison Industrial Complex, but I am a *Prisoner of the new Jim Crow?*

Chapter 1
To See A Prophet ≠ Profit

I was (4) years old when I saw murder for the first time. I don't remember the exact time or date, but I know it was during the day. My mother and I had just left my grandmother's house on North Avenue in West Baltimore. I don't even remember what our next destination was, whether we were headed home or wherever, but for as much as I can't recall, the moments that follow are branded into my brain. I'll never forget... my mother took me by the hand, and we jogged across the street, dodging traffic as we made our way to the bus stop at the end of the block. I remember, of all things trivial, that it was cold outside because we were standing somewhat huddled next to a payphone, and Mama was rubbing my hands in between hers to try and keep me warm. Suddenly, a long car came screeching to a halt in front of us and the other small multitude of people who stood waiting for the bus. Four men jumped out of the car and ran up the steps and into a row house on the immediate left side of the payphone we stood next to. I heard the sound of firecrackers for about (3) seconds, then nothing. Moments later, the four men emerged from the house, two of them escorting an old lady by her arms down the steps. The men hopped back into the long car and sped off, leaving the old lady standing in front of me. She had this look on her face like she was confused, and I can see two small holes on her cheek and side of her head that started to bleed. She had small red stains on her clothes, and I remembered that I couldn't take my eyes off her. She collapsed, and when she fell, she fell flat on her face right within arm's reach of me. I don't remember us moving away from her. I don't remember leaving the bus stop, but I remember the sound I heard from her face hitting the pavement. It was like the sound of a pumpkin or some large melon being smashed to the ground, like a pop, splatter, thud, all at the same time. Even as I'm writing this, that sound is echoing in my head. I wasn't frightened at the moment when all of this was happening. I just watched. I'm frightened by it all right now, but I don't recall any emotionalism from that day. I don't even know what Mama was doing or what any of the other people were doing or how anybody responded, but I know that I didn't see any police come through.

Knowing the world that I grew up in like I do, I can only imagine what chain of events led to this incident. The streets are wicked and spawn nothing short of wickedness. Good people who lack a strong constitution are lost to the evils of the streets every day. It's like one bad experiment after the other in one massive field test that's gone wrong, but the wrong is centered in the idea of, "What's the worst that could happen?" I've seen and oftentimes been a part of or a party to the thing where we're going to get together and have a good time, never considering, "What's the worst that could happen?", when seemingly out of the blue, a good time came at the expense of someone's pride, dignity, integrity, humanity or worse. It's like the streets can sense your vulnerabilities, so that becomes your test, all day, every day. How you turn out is a result of how you prepare, but how, or better yet, why would you prepare if you don't know you're being tested?

Good people who have a strong constitution are lost to the evils of the evils, of the wickedness of the streets every day. I'm sure someone out there would say that what I just said is an excuse for people who are too lazy, too passive, or too afraid to challenge and/or change their circumstances for the better. I'd say to that, that in some cases, maybe that's an accurate assertion. But I'd also say that such an assertion is an oversimplification of a complicated set of circumstances that usually is voiced by those who don't come from where I come from, nor have they ever been there to know the dynamics; so they're spouting off opinions, valid or not, as observers and not active participants. How dare you exclaim and brag about how you're from the hood or lived in the ghetto, because clearly you weren't in the streets, or you'd show a little more empathy towards the people who are entrenched in street people's problems. Let me be very clear... just because you're from the hood doesn't mean you're from the streets. It is a very distinct difference.

Please do not misunderstand me here. Being from the streets, as I've mentioned, is nothing to brag about. Those conditions and circumstances are absolutely fucking miserable, so the priority and the plight is to find a way up out of that shit, by whatever means that becomes available from one moment to the next. Nobody signs up for that kind of life; you're either born into it or conditioned into it. Meaning that, if you weren't born into it, a process of erosion and degradation has taken place where certain elements were lost in the state of chaos you found yourself trying to wade through. These last elements vary from person to person and family to family, but they were lost because someone was being overwhelmed by their circumstances.

For those who don't know, that savage arena is constantly changing, constantly modifying, and mutating. We don't adjust well to such drama, so we adopt a warped sense of survivalism that is only as good as the times, circumstances, and conditions such a mentality is fostered in. Once a change is introduced, that prior mentality becomes obsolete to the front runners of the day, which becomes the next generation of survivalists. A changing of the guard is fundamental to our growth and advancement as a community. Still, if the new guardian doesn't respect the ideas, lessons, and principles that are the foundation of the platform they now sit upon, we will digress instead of advancing. In this case, we found ourselves as savages in pursuit of happiness, blissfully ignorant and gradually moving away from nobility; the next generation, the now generation, is quickly becoming the worst that could happen because my contemporaries and I weren't there to guide them with what lessons we did learn. They had nothing to follow, no blueprint, no road map. They are the seeds of the digital world, while everything we could have given them was analog. They can only do what they know with what they have, and they have nothing because we, the old guard, weren't there. We were trying to survive and failed miserably because the streets are undefeated in this war, and we couldn't grasp the odds. We just couldn't see it.

I stated above that we weren't there. To grasp any of the concepts I'm laying out now, you have to think of this in the context of warfare. I've alluded to it a few times already, but you have to take it there if you want to understand. Also, you must consider that there is an entire faction of active participants in this war that don't even know that this is their reality. In war, you have casualties, fatalities. Some soldiers are killed in action (K.I.A.), some are missing in action (M.I.A.), some are captured by the enemy and become prisoners of war (P.O.W.), some just go (A.W.O.L.), absent without leave. So, when I say we weren't there, all of these above mentioned are interchangeable conditions from person to person, but all of them apply. They apply to an entire generation. Think about that. This isn't rhetorical. This isn't metaphorical or allegorical. In my neighborhood, I can count on my hands how many of my homeboys that I grew up with and actually hung-out and partied with, who are still alive and not either in prison or on parole or probation. What this means is that the rest of us are locked up, dead, or serving out the remainder of a sentence while on parole or probation, and this is just my immediate circle of friends and my extended circle of friends who ventured out into the deep end. Imagine, if you will, that in the city, one as small as Baltimore, you have a conglomeration of neighborhoods divided up just according to zip codes, then divide those zip codes up into zones and divide those zones up into a comfort radius where people tend to congregate. In East Baltimore, my personal comfort radius consisted of (11) separate neighborhoods. Still, you have to take into account that in Baltimore, our idea of a neighborhood is immediate and may only consist of anywhere from one city block to (5) before you're outside of the comfort radius.

In my comfort radius, (98%) of us were actively engaged on a physical level, but we were oblivious, in a very real sense, to the thing that we were engaged with. Thus, (100%) of us were mentally or intellectually inactive out of sheer ignorance, which typically made us more dangerous to ourselves and less of a threat to our enemy. To this very day, my neighborhood is a hotbed of crime and violence, which is an extension of poverty, illiteracy, pollution, intercommunal disenfranchisement and disconnectedness, and an extreme lack of self-awareness. With that comes a slew of social diseases that incite behaviors that show how our opponents justify our treatment politically and economically. In theory, the logical course of action that should be taken to steer this class of people in a more progressive and productive direction is to flood these debilitated communities with endless resources. The practice has been the exact opposite. Every past generation can and will readily attest to the disintegration of the communal ideas and the practices of those ideas out of shared communal interest. They don't talk about the root cause of the disintegration, which from one aspect is the erosion of the relationships that existed as a result of political-community interest and support.

The socio-cultural political makeup has transmuted into something unfamiliar. Socially and culturally, we've allowed ourselves to entertain an individualistic idea of how we should operate, so much so that our ability to maintain control over our community's development and advancement is a thing of the past. Our communities are now in politicians' hands that we don't know, that don't know us, and law enforcement. When I was home, it had gotten to the point where people couldn't sit out on their own stoop, let alone stand out in front of their own homes without being harassed by the police. But here's the thing, the double-edged sword of it, was that the drug culture was easing its way into areas that at one time were off-limits to such activities. Yeah, those areas where we lived. Here's what happened... In Baltimore, as I'm sure it is in any city in the world, all of the most illicit activities occur in the busiest and most brightly lit areas, so we had open-air drug markets, prostitution, and so forth in places like Pennsylvania Avenue, Park Heights, Greenmount Avenue, (25th) Street, etc. Periodically, there'd be sweeps conducted by law enforcement, where large groups of people would be indicted according to information gathered concerning their activities or associations in those areas. Spots start to receive too much attention from the police, so illicit activities migrate to places that aren't hot. If my original base of operations was in Lafayette Projects, if it got too hot for me to operate there, I simply go across the tracks, so to speak, and hustle my wares in Flag House Projects. However, in doing so, I have, more than likely, affectively left my comfort radius and ventured into someone else's, which creates tension due to the stress and anxiety of the people who now have to be concerned about the heat I have potentially brought with me into their comfort radius. Those concerns aren't only those of the other hustlers I'm now competing with, but also of the residents in those areas who might not even know me and would be less likely to receive me graciously and create a safe haven for me there. Over me, they'd choose the evil that they know.

Now, due to my invasion, the potential for beef is rising. I feel the tension and apprehension around my presence because I'm not welcome, and so with that comes an immediate need to be able to defend myself and/or ward off any advances that may jeopardize my enterprise, so I obtain a gun or guns for myself and anyone aligned with me. The police are aware of the temperament and alerted to any change of the temperament in the area(s) they patrol, so they react to the change with how they were trained. They step up their assertiveness and become more aggressive in how they engage the people within that area. This is supposed to be proactive, crime preventive measures that translate into,...

"What are you doing out here?"

"I'm sitting on my steps."

"Show me some ID."

"For what? I live here."

"Up against the wall! Hands-on your head!"

"For what? I didn't do nuthin!"

... which oftentimes escalates, which may lead to an arrest. More of this and these types of situations occur due to a severe lack of effective communication on both sides of that coin; but as a civilian who is being engaged by the police, the authorities own the obligation of being the consummate professional in this discourse. Fair or not, the uniform is symbolic of a brand of empirical authoritarianism, where what has become typical is the jadedness of the police toward the people and the fear and anxiety of the people toward the police. No one side trusts the other, and it's like that because neither side is invested in the other. No one can see beyond their emotionalism to see the humanity in each other, so there's static.

We don't believe in the police; the police, in our minds, has taken on the role of bounty hunters, vigilantes, and gangstas, while in their minds, it reflects that they see us and regard us as an annoyance in the least, but more so, as the worst that could happen when you give niggas/niggers too much leeway. Of course, this isn't the rule of thumb. Not everybody feels this way on either side, but if you take a consensus right now for (2019) in the urban industrial and residential base, if (35%) of that population doesn't have faith in their town's police, that's too many, way too many. Quite naturally, that number was a generous estimation and illustration, especially for Baltimore City.

We don't feel like we have the faith of the police or the politicians because our experiences with law enforcement weren't the most wholesome. How did we go from meeting Officer Friendly to Officer Friendly and his partner, taking me to a secluded area and beating me half to death? The situation is intense because of the criminalization of a poverty-stricken class born out of a desire to capitalize politically and economically off of poor people's problems and the mechanisms we employ to cope with life as we know it, and because of media hype that sensationalizes human degradation. I'm highly critical of the media because of the lack of objectivity. Objectivity doesn't get the ratings; it doesn't grab attention. What gets the most attention is disaster, fear, chaos, turmoil, and tumultuousness. The stories that show off the best of people's character in the spirit of unity, redemption, and peace come on within the last (30) seconds of the broadcast. Where is the balance in that?

I'm highly critical of politicians because they have and use the power to direct human affairs with the policies they make that the authorities enforce. The policymakers established the rules that govern our interactions, then wait for the rules to be compromised and create new safeguards to protect the old rules from being subjected to their own exceptions. Thus, we get amended rules that even they can't determine how a person or people will respond or react to the vast array of situations we tend to call life. The policymakers direct traffic and control the flow of our day-to-day comings and goings, how we deal with one another, how we take care of ourselves with the access we have to public resources, and what information we receive concerning the social paradigm. We subscribe to a political process that, in theory, is supposed to represent the best interests of its citizenship. The economic backdrop of this political process is capitalism, which again, in theory, would support democracy, but for the fact that we live under a democracy through representation. The fatal flaw in a capitalist society is that it functions through a socio-economic, socio-cultural, and socio-political caste that, by sheer design, must maintain a permanent underclass. What this means is that the people's access is determined by their cultural and economic station. Those situated at the bottom of the social ladder in this society are never truly represented under this form of democracy and are more prone to be subjected to social diseases than those who can afford better. Those who can afford better have a much louder voice in the policymaking process. Typically, laws are made and passed in response to how poor people react to being poor, not as a means through which to solve poor people's problems.

We find ourselves at the mercy of these politicians who idealize the spectrum of the human drama that becomes the cultural and political landscape through which we must navigate. We usually make our decisions based on the condition of the terrain, which changes with the weather. As much as we may try to exercise vigilance, prudence, and consideration, we don't always make the best moves in the clutch when we are at our best. That said, some consequences are attached to our indecisiveness, indiscretions, and shallow thinking; so we elect from within the collective representatives who have the unique ability to articulate our vision of our ideal world, analyze our overall dilemmas to bring ease to our development and resolve our collective grievances judiciously. Such practices are abandoned regarding the destitute, and as a result, an entire multitude of people are held in check because they simply can't access many of the resources that are fundamental to their personal and interpersonal well-being. Much of that access is systematically denied. Deprivation creates desperation, which leads to exasperation. This is a psychological and physiological perfect storm that no one is equipped to weather. Thus, the immediate concern is not chasing rainbows while everything we have is getting washed away. It's virtually impossible for one to find calm whilst staying in the mists of calamity, but calamity is a constant for poor people. Breaking the law could eventually become an option. Often, it seemed like the only option, but still, this is no excuse. We can't tolerate intolerable behavior. We only have these options: accept or don't accept one's reasoning for dealing in the low, complain, grieve, hold a grudge, seek penance, forgive, understand, or don't, if that gives you peace of mind; but, realize this situation is very complex. What do you do when you are at your wits end trying to find solutions to your issues, and the good people who are charged with the task of maintaining and perpetuating social harmony are found to be complicit in promoting and executing policies that deepen your angst? Now really, who am I to be critical of any-one? I'm just one out of a couple of million people who, for almost (2 ½) decades, has been the living, breathing embodiment of an amended rule. I was (4) years old when I saw murder for the first time...

Chapter 2
Mind Your Business

My sense of smell is horrible. I had developed allergies to pollen, cut grass, dust, and seemingly good weather at around (10) years old. I was diagnosed with sinusitis, which directly impacted my ability to smell unless the aroma was simply overwhelming or right under my nose. I get a sick feeling in the pit of my stomach every time I smell Pine-Sol or pine-scented disinfectants and cleaning chemicals. Every time that scent is in the air, I immediately get nauseous and strangely exhausted, almost like my body is telling me that I need sleep. In my lifetime, that scent was never as present but for two occasions, entering *Steel Side* in the Baltimore City Detention Center and again as I made my way into the Maryland House of Corrections, *the Cut*, as it was called.

Say what you want but, nothing in this life can prepare you mentally, physically, or spiritually, to be chained and shackled, number one, and number two, to be ushered into a cage that measures approximately (12-15 ft wide, 8-10 ft long), and I can't even remember how high, with one bench, a toilet and (20 to 25) other men. We are shoulder to shoulder; some of us are stretched out on the floor, posted up on the grill, or curled up in a ball of our own filth. We've just come from our first court appearance being told by a judge the ransom demand for our freedom, or what they call "Bail Review," which for the upwards of (97%) of us can't afford, so it effectively has put all of us on no-bail status. Most of us haven't bathed in at least (24) hours. Two-thirds of us are still coming down off the drugs and alcohol, *illin'* (dope-sick). All of us are tired and bewildered, and for a first-timer like me, scared shitless, literally. The air is filled with a mixture of B.O., fecal matter, dragon-breath, vomit, urine, smuggled tobacco, some female officer's ultra-strong perfume, and my old friend, pine-scented, blackened mop water with a mildewed mop. It's loud from all of the recidivists yelling back and forth from one bullpen to the other, trying to holla' at a homeboy to send word to the section they just recently were released from, in an attempt to get sent over a care package of sorts to get started on this particular journey. There's no rest for the weary. Everybody is looking for a familiar face, preferably a friendly face, to ease the anxiety that comes with the territory.

I'm surrounded by the people whom I had the least amount of respect for out in the streets; dope-fiends and crackheads, you know, junkies, with their swollen hands and twitchy behavior. They stink. They keep farting and shitting and throwing up and breathing. I can hear their conversations, how they got jammed up in a dope hole with the dudes that had the smack on some random strip. I hear them mapping out where they want to go to be housed in the jail; what top-shelf hustler or *Head-Bussa'* is on what sections; I hear them plotting the move and the next move after that, and all I can do is sit there, shoulder to shoulder with these funky mutha' fuckas' waiting on Lord knows what to happen next because I don't have a clue. Some old city jail vet eventually starts to talk about the routine we're about to follow, mentioning the slight inconveniences we may have to deal with as the jail has to make accommodations for our stay...

"Y'all know this shit is over-crowded in here, so them Mu' Fuckas gon' make us sleep in the school trailer tonight and then tomorr' we gon' over and sleep in the gym. Shit, we gon' be movin' 'round like that all week 'til they find us some bed space on Receivin'. They got niggas up in the gym sleepin' in them new plastic boats and shit."

He was right. For the first five days, I spent in that jail, I couldn't sleep, I had no appetite, and we moved every night from one nasty spot where we were supposed to sleep to another. No showers. No phone calls. No friends and family around to talk to, just a bunch of junkies who didn't mind sharing their cigarettes. I couldn't use the bathroom in there, and although I constantly feel like I'm about to throw up, that won't even come out of me. It's like I was shutting down a part of myself to be opened up to something else.

That was a set of circumstances in these first few days, unlike anything I could have ever imagined, and this was only the beginning. My first cell was on C-section, which was the "Receiving" section of the jail. The tier was run by this militant bald-headed black officer, who woke up everybody on his section as soon as his shift started. "Top of the morning, top of the morning, top of the morning!" After that loudness, if you don't wake up, it's because you can't wake up. For me, on that first morning, it was just more of the same, a rude, very intrusive awakening. I didn't formally meet my cage-mate until lunchtime. As soon as my feet hit the floor, I lit a Newport, smoked it down a little past halfway, and then passed it to the dude wrapped up in beige tinted sheets on the bottom bunk. I took a leak, threw some water on my face, and lit another cigarette. The lunch trays came about an hour later. City jail special brown and green bologna, which everybody called *"Sweaty Betty"*, some cold but funny looking potato salad, and a cup of this colored water they told me was called "Base." All of a sudden, my cage-partner got up and went to the grill. He started yelling, "Working Man!" "Working Man!" One of the guys that apparently was responsible for handing out the lunch trays came over to the cell. "Yo, where the fuck is my dessert?!" He turned to me and asked, "Did your tray have some dessert?" I told him no. He turned his focus back to the working man and told him, "Yo, go get our shit!" "Who the fuck you think you playing wit'?" "Go get our fuckin' dessert, nigga!" The dude looked up at me and told my cage partner, "Chill, Black. I got you. I'll be right back." He left and came back in maybe a minute with a handful of oatmeal pies. By that time, I climbed off the bunk and was sitting on the toilet/sink. Black counted out (20) oatmeal pies and gave me (10). "My name is Black. These niggas be stealin' the cookies and *Debbies* off the trays, tryin' to carry a nigga to the left.

If you get a breakfast tray, make sure your sugar is on it. Lunch and dinner is supposed to have *Debbies*, cookies, or cake. If that shit ain't on there, check them niggas, or they gon' think you's a bitch and you ain't never gon' eat." He stuck out his swollen, crusty, black hand; I shook it and told him, "Good lookin' out, my name is O."

I stayed in that cell for two weeks with Black, and for the whole 2 weeks, all we did was smoke, laugh, trade war stories, and hold class on jailhouse etiquette. Rule #1) "Don't be the *Lick*." If you listen more than you talk, niggas can't figure you out, so they'll focus their energy on something else. Remain humble and respect the hunger of a mutha' fucka' who never had a full stomach. Rule #2) "Respect everything." Respect begets respect. Have some respect for yourself, for others, and your surroundings. Do not tolerate disrespect. Even if you think you might lose the fight, as long as you stand up for yourself, niggas gonna' honor that. The first time you allow a nigga to disrespect, it's no coming back from that until you fuck around and kill one of these worthless ass niggas. Then you're stuck. Rule #3) "Mind your mutha' fuckin' business." Everything else came naturally under those three things, so I never clicked up, I never explored my vices, and I never bragged about what I was doing on the street. I fell into obscurity, and unless you knew me, you didn't even know I was there.

After those two weeks were up, I got moved into a (50) man dormitory. The first day I was in there, one of the two other dudes that came over with me checked-in. He never even unpacked his property or even made his bed. I was assigned to a bunk in the center of the dorm along a row on the back about (15) beds long. I basically can see every inch of the dorm from my area, so I saw when the dude went to the front of the dorm, which is the day room area, and waved down the C.O... After he spoke to the officer, he never went back to his bunk area. The officer opened the gate, the dude walked out, and the C.O. put handcuffs on him. He was gone. Two C.O.'s came into the dorm a few minutes later and packed up whatever property he had left that wasn't pillaged. About an hour or so later, this tall dude, I didn't know, made his way over to me and asks, "Main-Man, why'd ya' homeboy check-in?" Immediately I knew I was being sized up. I stood up, look the dude in his eyes, and said, "I don't know that nigga." He stood there for about two seconds and then walked away. After he did so, I went into the bathroom-shower area, which was cornered off by a large plastic curtain. I made sure to shut the curtain behind me, walked into the furthest corner, took a couple of deep breaths, and waited. I waited, and I waited, but no one came. Realize that at the time, I'm (18) years old, I might weigh about (140) pounds, standing at almost (6'4). I'm a twig, which is the story of my life, and I gotta' be ready to go when it's go-time, which again, is the story of my life. I don't have anyone to back me up, I have no weapons to help my cause, but if this is what it is, then that's what is simply has to be. Don't take this as if I'm trying to sound tough. I was scared out of my goddamned mind, not knowing what may be about to happen to me. I had never been locked-up before. I'm just flying by the seat of my pants, instinctively doing what I can to preserve my existence, but I didn't really know what I was doing. In the days that follow, my powers of observation were put to the test as I started to realize who was who and what made this particular spot shake. It was definitely guys that were clicked up, but it was weird. The dorm broke down into the following groups... the first and seemingly most influential was the prayer circle, which consisted of about (10) guys and led by Big Jim, a huge white boy from *Pig Town*, that looked like he ate the weights he supposed to be lifting. His right-hand man was a black dude they called Two-Slice. As I was told, Two-Slice got his name because he came into the jail, a crackhead who was skinnier than me but got his weight up from going around asking everybody for their bread at every meal. When I first saw the brotha', he had to weigh at least (200) pounds, easy. These guys prayed hard and loud, every day and every night, with enough conviction to command that the other (40) of us maintain quietly while they recite the Lord's Prayer. The second group was a random bunch of about

(6) guys who simply ran wild. It didn't seem like they followed anyone in particular, but these dudes were always in the midst of a plot unfolding, always in a huddle, and none of them ever seemed to have anything of their own. They try to bogart all four of the phones, all of the good seats in the dayroom when something good was on T.V., and they were always flashing a knife, making a knife, or trying to find a good stash for their knives. They were like hyenas; they did more scavenging than hunting, but once they got on your ass, survival was a slim chance. I had already figured out that if I ever had any static with these dudes, my best chance was to isolate the strongest one from the rest of his pack and dig in his chest 'til I struck gold. I had to use everything I learned on the street to my advantage; stealth, intelligence, intimidation, and my ability to seize the moment to maximize controlled chaos and my explosive output to cause as much damage as my little ass could muster. I'm glad it never came to that. The other groups were splinters of sorts. They were made up of guys who enjoyed a good smoke and good conversation. Anybody could fit in depending on what brand of cigarettes you prefer, how early you woke up in the morning, and how late you stayed up at night.

The longer I stayed in the jail in general and the dorm in particular, going back and forth to court, going on passes to medical, visitation, and skating around the jail, a common theme started to resonate that was duplicitous. Seniority is everything in that place; the longer you stay, the more access you gain, the more respect you'd receive, that's number one. The flip side of that was that those dope-fiends and crackheads had the run of the city jail. They owned it. They were apart of everything, and everything in that jail went through them; the drugs, the cash, the women, you name it. As my popularity grew amongst these guys, I was exposed to more of the world I was living in, but I was never compelled to click up with anybody. I felt safer on my own. When I think about it, I guess I always have. Nevertheless, the rewards I received just for me, being myself, were tremendous regarding where I found myself. Of course, I can't say that for everyone.

As I mentioned earlier, I came into the dorm with two other guys, one of which checked-in within minutes of our arrival. The other dude, he was something else. He and I never really got on the same page. He was really into getting with whatever was moving for the moment. Whoever was in play, this dude would try to fit in with that. I couldn't vibe with that energy. He reminded me of one of those kids from school who wants so badly to be a part of the in-crowd and would take on the characteristics of a bully if it meant that he was accepted. To me, that's always been a sign of weakness. Such behaviors are seriously time-barred, and when the clock expires, all bets are off. The dude called himself June Bug. June Bug had started trying to edge his way into that wild pack of hyenas by being *extra*. They started to insert him into their activities by getting him to hold their knives. He started getting louder by the day and bolder by the minute. On my end, the older, more confident, and calmer gentlemen would find me and put me up on *game*. Because of the arena, *game* was always more cerebral in content than one being able to play Dominos, Spades, or Monopoly. They were teaching me Chess, Checkers, and Pinochle. In Chess, the most important elements were knowing all of the pieces and how they move; knowing the board or the landscape; being able to visualize the process of controlling the board, which means that I can dictate the moves of my opposition; but most of all, being able to visualize my path to victory. In Checkers, everything is about what angles your opponent is taking; being able to limit or prohibit them from taking those angles they prefer; understanding the virtues that come from a righteous sacrifice, and not being afraid to make the correct sacrifices at the proper time despite the odds. Pinochle is about sowing seeds for the harvest. June Bug was a pawn. His only aspiration was to be whatever someone else determined he should be for them. He was easily manipulated and ripe to be sacrificed. It had come to a point where it was discovered that someone was stealing in the dorm, which is among the worst violations of the prison code and the *G-Code*. The penalty for stealing could range from a vicious beating and ostracism, being beaten, stabbed, ostracized, and possibly killed. Thieves received no mercy upon being caught, and the most pious brothers from amongst us didn't hesitate to join in the fray when the time came to execute the penalty upon a thief. That's possibly due to these pious brothers being victimized by that thief simply because of their non-threatening disposition; you know, the taking one's kindness for weakness thing. The dorm was in an uproar. The thing is, it's (50) of us, so there'll never be a time when (49) of us are all asleep, and the thief is the only person up and about. Someone will see something that he may not want to see or isn't supposed to see, so a thief ideally will be fronted. Sometimes prison politics are afoot, and someone who may indeed be the thief has enough influence to create a vicious misdirection campaign, where some innocent fool gets the blame, and the penalty, while the wolf continues to hide amongst the sheep.

In this case, the hyenas, as I've taken to calling them, are at the helm, spearheading the investigation into this mystery. They're making threatening announcements, going into people's bunk areas searching for the stolen goods, and me, while this is going on, I have arrived at my own conclusion. Since the first incident was brought out, the hyenas had been eating commissary that I knew they didn't have. These dudes lived off the land, none of them ever got any mail, so they didn't receive money orders, which excludes them from going to the store. They didn't go on visits to smuggle in the goods they could use to hustle up commissary, so in my mind, it's a simple deduction, either the hyenas did it, convinced someone else to do it, or ol' June Bug is dumber than I gave him credit for. Either way, the hyenas are in on the *lick*, and putting on a show of outrage and being loud and obnoxious about this situation is just a smokescreen. I suspected that these weirdos were setting the stage for something dramatic to happen. Remember, I had the good fortune of sleeping dead center, so again, I can see the whole dorm in front of me, and what I see are constant secret conversations going on between the prayer circle, the hyenas, and a few concerned vets. For whatever reason, Big Jim, Two-Slice, and a dude I often talk to named Ace, called me over to the bathroom. When I walked in, Ace motioned for me to pull the curtain closed, and Two-Slice walked over to make sure nobody came walking into our conversation, so basically, he held the position of security. Ace went into his *dip* and brandished an ugly rusty looking piece of metal. He said, "Take this. We know who's been stealin' and it's getting handled. Don't keep this in your bunk area, and don't have it on you unless you plan on using it. If you have to use it, make sure I'm on point so somebody can watch ya' back." I'm looking at this rusty makeshift blade, not knowing what to think, when Big Jim interjects, "O, we bought you in here 'cause you're one of the good ones. You're going to be ok. We want you to know that we got your back if shit goes south." They showed me where they keep all their knives, and I was obliged to place mines amongst the rest. It had to be (30) random pieces of steel in that spot, but me, thinking the way I do, thought in that very instant about what happens on the street when a stash house gets raided, usually, you take a hefty loss, so a rule of thumb is never to place all of your eggs in one basket. So, I didn't. I held onto the blade, studied it in a way, the sharpness of the point in ratio to the edge, its weight, the width, even the wrap of the handle. I'm standing there thinking, "This mutha' fucka' ain't even sharp.", and while I'm thinking and just being in my head about what to do with this thing, I hear the squeaks of multiple shoes on the floor and the screech and groans of metal legs being violently shifted out of their natural positioning. I hear the thud of bodies hitting the floor, and I soon noticed the normal dorm chatter had ceased completely. Then I hear, "Yo, chill! Yo, chill! Come on, man! Chill!" In the moment and off pure instincts, I went towards the bathroom curtain and was stopped short by Ace and Big Jim. The commotion lasted for a few minutes, and once it settled, the four of us emerged from our safe haven.

Everybody was on their bunks. Everybody. Naturally, I

went directly to my bunk, looked around, and saw June Bug in his area looking absolutely disheveled. His shirt was torn half-way off, he had no shoes on his feet, and he was holding a rag to his face. Somebody yelled out, "Pack up, Bitch! June Bug looked up and hollered back, "Fuck y'all! Pack me up!" Everybody sat still for a little while longer, and then everything seemed to go back to business as usual. It's tense though, and even as people are doing everything they normally do, it looks like everybody is moving differently. It was like that for the next few hours. Then, it happened. Somewhere around (10:30) PM, just (30) minutes before shift change, June Bug decided he needed to use the bathroom. He went in, and not even (10) seconds later, the hyenas followed him. Big Jim, Two-Slice, and Ace called out for prayer, and as usual, the circle went in hard and loud with soulful conviction. ...

"Yea though I walk through the valley in the shadow of death, I will fear no evil! I will fear no evil! I will fear no evil!"

...That was the longest rendition of the Lord's Prayer I'd ever heard. The hyenas came out of the bathroom and quickly dispersed to their bunk areas, stripping down to their underwear as they went, throwing their discarded T-shirts and shorts or sweatpants to Big Jim, who put the clothes in the trash bag and passed the bag over to the dorm next to ours, where I learned that all of those items were destroyed and disposed of. June Bug never came out of that bathroom. Shift changed, and the officer conducted the count. Of course, when he checked the bathroom, he immediately got on his radio and shouted a code to alert staff as to his discovery. We were all made to stay in our bunk areas while June Bug was rushed out to be treated for injuries. Through all of this, I'm lying on my bunk, processing everything that's happening, the hyenas are all playing sleep, nobody's really saying too much in terms of conversation, and it dawned on me, I'm still holding this dumb-ass knife. As it would happen, a team of C.O.'s rushed into the dorm and commits to search our areas for weapons and/or evidence related to June Bug's assault. I'm scared to death now because I can't just get up and hide the shit, and I don't know what to do. I started looking around to see if there was any move I could make to get this thing off me and avoid the blame for the incident with June Bug. As the C.O.'s closed in, it dawned on me now to pay attention to how they moved. They started searching the back of the dorm, then collapsed to the front of the dorm, leaving the center for last. I motioned to Ace, who slept in the back, and basically let him know that I was holding. My thoughts were, if I could slip to the back of the dorm, someone else could move to my bunk area, and we'd switch until the shakedown was over. Ace was my man, it's like he was reading my mind, and within seconds we made our move. His area was already searched, so I went as far as to get under the sheets and played possum until the C.O.'s left. I never saw June Bug again, and I never found out to what extent he was hurt. This was the first time I had ever seen an incident of this caliber in this setting, but it certainly was far from being the last.

I stayed in that dorm long enough to see the turnover of the population there. Some guys finally made bail, some got time and wound up going into the system, some went home due to court releases of some sort, but very rarely did someone outright beat their case. Many of the more popular guys were moving on, but for every single person that left, their spot was filled immediately. The impact of the guys leaving varied according to who left. For example, three of the hyenas were packed up within days of each other, which had an immediate impact on the dorm's culture. Two-Slice went home, and from there, a lot changed as well. It was like the heart and soul of the dorm had started to be siphoned away. Truth be told, it was not fun anymore; it wasn't as alive. I came to realize that the thing that kept us invigorated was the action, the constant feeling that trouble was brewing, and then seeing the plays as they were being executed. I've seen men getting tied down to their bunks while they were asleep and awakened by someone beating their face in with the head of a push broom. I've seen men run naked, wet, and bleeding, from the shower, being chased around the dorm by other men with dull makeshift knives. We had a small riot at one point, where we were bucking against being served stroganoff for three days straight because they kept running out of food when it came time to feed our dorm. We actually had to come together in a standoff against the Goon Squad. These are some of the largest human beings working in corrections. You will never see them until it's time to fuck somebody up, and once they're called in, usually it's no turning back. When this all started, of course, collectively, we were angry as hell. It was supposed to be chicken for dinner, with mashed potatoes, gravy, and string beans; the one night of the week when we get a break from all of the soybean-based, meat-like, cheap bullshit they've been stuffing us full of for (6) days, at three meals a day. We just wanted our one meal, not some flavorless noodles, brown sauce, and ground soy meat that they've had stuffed in the freezer, thawed out (15) minutes ago, barely reheated, and have served us for a third straight day. All (50) of us came into the dining hall that barely seated (30) people and refused to take our trays, and we refused to leave the area until we got our chicken dinner.

A Captain was called in to diffuse the situation, but he wasn't very receptive to our plight, so we asked for a Major, who, when he came, was even less on board with listening to our complaint, that we felt was absolutely legitimate. He called in the Goons. They came in suited and booted in head-to-toe riot gear; shields, helmets, flak jackets, Billy clubs, the whole nine. We were locked in the dining room, where we could see through the window of the officer's bubble that the dining room was being surrounded. At that point, we had some decisions to make. The question was asked, "Who wants to leave?" No one spoke up. We all agreed that if someone decided to leave, it wouldn't be held against them; as a group, we'd understand. No one spoke up. Everyone stayed, and we knew at that point that it was going down; we just didn't know how. Time was elapsing, and, in my mind, we were in that dining room for what seemed like forever. The Major, who at some point made his way into the officer's bubble, opened up a small slot that allowed communication between us in the dining room and the officers in the bubble and gave us all instruction to remove our shoes, line up single file, starting at the dining room entrance and exit door and step out of the dining room, one at a time with our hands over our heads. No one moved. More time lapsed. We sat, we stood, we stretched and milled about, but no one said a word, that is, until some tall man in a shirt and tie get-up, a pair of slacks and *Slippery Earls*, came fast walking his way into the bubble. You could tell he was some kind of a boss, and by his body language, you could see that he was well beyond irate. This brother was mad as shit. His hands were all over the place as he looked to be barking at the Major and the Captain, who made their way into the bubble behind the tall man. After a few minutes of that exchange, he left the bubble and made his way into the dining room, escorted by the Captain. "What's the problem?" No one said a word. He looked around at us, then pulled out his walkie-talkie, gave the command, and we watched as the Goons filed out. "Now, what's the problem?" Big Jim spoke up, which really was only right since, technically, he started all this shit. Once the door was open and the dialogue began, it was like the floodgates flew open, and we let out all our grievances as the tall man took notes. We aired out everything, how slow the mail is coming and going in and out; how we have broken phones that leave (50) people fighting over the use of the only two that are semi-operational; how we haven't been to the gym in over a month because the C.O.'s "don't feel like" sending us; broken toilets, rodents, broken showers and sinks, everything we can think of. By the time the conversation was over, the brother's notepad had a nice long bucket list. I don't think any of us even remember that we hadn't eaten until the tray slots suddenly slammed open. The tall man stood up and made his way to the door and waved and said, "Enjoy your meal."

"Lord have mercy!" When we got our trays, everybody had two pieces of chicken with the pile of those instant mashed potatoes drowning in gravy, and a big ol' slice of cake. They even let us go back for more until the food was gone. Riot turn feast. Well, not quite a riot, but we were definitely at the cusp of one. The prayer circle blessed the meal; we feasted and rode high for the rest of the night. Out of all that was expressed, the phones got fixed, and we got more gym recreation, but nothing else, at least for the rest of the time I was there. Truth be told, the very few concessions that were made didn't all of a sudden create a utopian existence for us in that jail and especially not in the dorm, but we felt like we were heard and that for once, our voices were respected, even if only for a moment. It felt good to me. It made me feel important, strong. I later found out that that tall man was the Acting Assistant Warden.

Power is an incredible thing to have and to behold. In all the intellectual circles that I've traveled within, we have collectively discerned that power is the ability to define, defend, and promote one's best image and interests. The discernment is most important to those who are powerless and had no aspirations towards becoming powerful due to a severe lack of understanding that as a human being, one needs self-recognition to have the capacity to define and redefine reality based on their own worldview; one must have the ability to defend that reality, philosophy, perspective and worldview from intrusion and imposition; and, one must be able to promote their best image and interests as a means of perpetuating their existence and the integrity of their culture. This cannot be done through adaptation, assimilation, or being inculcated into a culture inconsistent with the socio-cultural, socio-political, and spiritual fabrics ingrained in a person or a people's DNA. It is by creative design and designation that you be who and what you are. To function and to behave as anything other than who and what you are, from the most extraordinary of perspectives, throws creation in its entirety into complete chaos. I feel like, right now, I need to go big into my analysis to show the true gravity of our collective situation. If my illustration fails to hit its mark at this point, I can and will downsize it all later, but bear with me...

...The universe is a member of creation that was fashioned

with such mathematical exactness that, if the earth were one millimeter off its axis, life as we know it could not exist. That is not to say that there'd be no life, just that as we perceive the phenomena, it would be absolutely different. Everything in creation is fashioned the same way. Creation perpetuates creation because of this. Thus, everything under the sun, everything under the thumb of creation has its own assignment, designation, and role that in its own right serves the collective purpose, to revolutionize and advance creation. Everything lives to provide a service to life. This is the be-all-end-all of it, like it or not, and really it's just that simple. This is our ordinance and how we perform this heavy task is through a process of empowerment. This is to embolden and strengthen one or a collective by facilitating ideas and ideals consistent with their growth and development, mentally, physically, spiritually, emotionally, economically, etc.

Nature is on board with this endeavor in its totality, so observing nature bears witness to what processes empower us to be and to become. The problem that we consistently run into is that man insists on pushing the parameters of the creative design, so much so, that as a result, abnormalities begin to find their way into the process. Now, if everything was made to instinctively empower everything else, where does oppression, suppression, and repression find a place in the natural scheme? The reality for an oppressed people is that life as we know it is contemptuous and constantly bordering on the fringes of disaster because someone is determined to maintain such an atmosphere. Part and parcel of this campaign to maintain oppression are to remove all the tangible and intangible elements that serve as tools of empowerment. How do you become that in which you don't know that you had the potential to be? Ask yourself, if you will, what innate forces compels you to be self-aware, self-determined, and do extraordinary things in opposition to such a thorough process of miseducation? I allude to miseducation to direct your focus to this point; the quality of life for poor people hinges upon education, and poor people are poorly educated. That is the standard for this society; thus, the quality of the education we receive is determined by the education we can afford. Also, the information that becomes the core of the education system is not customized to suit the educational needs of the individual to cultivate this one into the unique role that she or he was created to perform within as a servant to the rest of creation, that in turn serves her or him. On the contrary, the information is generalized to cultivate the general population all at once, which is a cost-effective way to assimilate, codify, and effectuate a herd mentality. This is the system, and this is how the system propels and perpetuates itself and how it has maintained itself for centuries now.

Think about how this works; the general rule is that everyone receives an equal education. How then do we explain the need for privatized schooling if public schooling is the equitable vehicle to induce our progeny? By all means, they are receiving the same information, right? Does information vary by quality? Do we distinguish between who receives the better-quality information? Of course, we do. The better the quality of the information better qualifies the informed. This is a society built on classism, which is supported by capitalism, which by nature and at its very core heralds the spirit of competition. Poor people are poorly equipped to compete and barely ever qualify for the competition. So again, what compels you? Information is disseminated according to class. We socialize and share this information amongst our classmates; thus, a continuous cycle persists from one generation to the next. Information is empowering, but education is powerful. In this regard, if one is educed with information in the service of the growth and the development of a foreign agency or someone not of your own race, class, or creed, the execution of the information is empowering to them, not to you and yours. Someone or something else gains from your lack of self-knowledge and self-determination; thus, you being miseducated and misinformed becomes the catalyst of your exploitation, which pushes the exploited to catapult those who oppress. While they are steadily being pushed forward, the oppressed class are steadily falling behind...you're behind in the rent, behind on the gas and electric bill, behind on the phone bill, behind on the medical bills, if you have a vehicle, you're behind on the car payment, behind on the vehicle insurance, you're behind on the water bill, it's a hole in the roof of the house, the plumbing is old and messed up... this shit gets deeper and deeper, which deepens your anxiety, deepens your depression. This is typical of the oppressed's worldview: pressure, constant pressure to keep up despite being held back. Excuses, right? Call it that if you want, but someone is living in this reality. In fact, someone has to. That's how this all works.

I'd like to take it a step further. How do we deal with anxiety, depression, hell, how do we deal with reality? Most people I know are looking for an escape, which is common amongst the rich and poor alike. This demands its own treatment because reality is subjective, so our escape routes will vary from person to person. In pursuit of a solution to our societal ills that are our own personal problems, some people rely on drugs, alcohol, some people exercise, some people clean, have sex, eat, it varies. For some, the reality persists, so they increase the intensity of their pursuit. Reality doesn't cease to be real despite its subjectivity, and so as it becomes more, the more the need to escape, the more intense the pursuit of that route. Some people can satisfy this supposed need with one vehicle through which they escape. My personal thing was weed, alcohol, sex, and my hustle, which was selling heroin and weed, not in any particular order. For many of us, the desire to escape became precipitous for our addictions. As human beings, we are hard-wired to be creatures of habit, so we do things habitually as a means of comprehending the success of our endeavors. If the objective is to feel good or receive a gratifying physical and mental sensation, then the objective is to find or create the means to achieve a dopamine release.

There aren't many glaring differences between addictions and obsessive-compulsive disorder. Of course, the physiological ramifications of, say, a heroin addiction versus the neuroticisms of a person who has an obsessive compulsion to clean is not the same. Still, psychosis is the main variation between the two, where both behaviors are definitively the same. I raise this because many of our addictions were born out of an obsession, and I had some of both. I had become obsessed with my desire to make money in the streets, but I became addicted to the lifestyle that came with making money in the streets; however, what I didn't realize that had eventually become apparent, was that this lifestyle came equipped with its own culture of death and destruction. I never thought that my reality included that I'd be arrested and sent to jail or even prison. It had never happened to me, so I never prepared myself for such an eventuality that is an integral part of the lifestyle I led. My fault. I felt that if I could make money, I could escape the depths of the anxiety and depression that comes with the pressure to keep up with the very same mutha' fuckas' who designed this system to protect themselves and their world from being intruded upon by a little nigga like me. Everybody around me was behind and kept coming up short. We were coming up so short that we totally lost focus and forgot what we were up against, so we inverted our energies and started to compete against one another. In all, none of us could win because doing so would contradict the overall design; thus, we have to believe that the virtual and conceptual limitations that come with miseducation and/or being poorly educated and misinformed are real and that we shall not overcome or even deeper still, that we already have and this is the most we should expect to gain from this life; the effect of which renders us powerless. We are powerless when we subscribe to the rules of the *game*; powerless when we limit ourselves to the information provided us instead of investigating and coming to our own realizations; powerless when we don't see ourselves as just as much of a significant force in this life as all of the rest of creation; and, powerless when we embrace the deranged idealisms that classify us and defines us as niggers/niggas.

What compels you? In city jail, I was furnished with information from Black that empowered my instincts and intuition to survive within that terrain. Big Jim and Two-Slice, on the surface, were empowered by their faith, which for them was a survival tactic. The hyenas were empowered by the idea of there being strength in numbers. June Bug was empowered by the idea of social acceptance from the same pack mentality of the hyenas that fostered his behavior. It all became a matter of style at the end of the day, but in the final analysis, we all at some point and in some way needed one another to achieve the one goal we all shared in common, ... to maneuver, manipulate, navigate and ultimately survive the day with what we're equipped with, which in this case, was next to nothing.

I was released after (7) months, one day, after my (19th) birthday, and all I could talk about, every word that came out of my mouth began with, "When I was over the jail, ..." I started to equate the principles of survival I learned in that dismal place to the realities I had to face out in the streets. The way I viewed the world was different. My approach to the *game* was more refined. I was refined. I asserted myself so much more, and I was much more aggressive. All that empowering information I had gathered and added into my personal arsenal helped me so much when I got arrested (2) months later and went back to the city jail...

Chapter 3
Check the Trade

I hated school growing up. You know, the more I reflect on it, it wasn't so much that I actually hated school; I really deeply disliked schooling. In elementary, if I showed up with a *C* on my report card, that was the surest route to an ass whipping. That being said, by the fourth quarter, I had to pass with nothing less than a *B* average to avoid that belt. Fortunately for me, that type of drama only lasted up until my mother and father separated while I was in the third grade. Don't get me wrong; I still couldn't blow off getting decent grades and passing to the next grade up. It's just that those heavy-handed lashings from the old man were across town and not just a room apart. Of course, since he was gone, that level of fear and anxiety subsided just enough for my work ethic to start to take a steady yet gradual decline. This isn't to say that my mother didn't kick ass or that her discipline didn't carry as much weight as my father's, because it did, but since he rolled out, she became the primary breadwinner... the only bread-winner. Now, she has to work, and she's working two jobs, so she was gone a lot. As a result, my productivity became less because the system that manifested the checks and balances in our house was completely out of whack. Thus, like any other kid in my posi-tion, I noticed the change in the atmosphere long before I noticed or could comprehend the impact. As a result, I, just like every kid in the same position sometimes created opportunities to take ad-vantage of the situation. I stopped doing homework, and by the time I reached the eighth grade, I wasn't even bringing my school-books home. Nevertheless, every year I passed with above-aver-age grades. I'm not quite sure what kept getting me through. My recollection of what went through my mind during certain classes, such as math, science, and social studies, always leads me to a blank space. My favorite subjects were art, reading, and physical education. I hated math because I couldn't understand fractions. I never did a science project and social studies, well, I could never get past the *dramacidal* nature of the people we were told to give reverence to, such as the founding fathers of the United States of America. It always confused me, the amount of conflict that entrenched the world we were learning about with its specific cast of characters, who seemed to be intent on pursuing anti-social living conditions at every turn. What I mean is that history is riddled in conflict, war, and what I couldn't wrap my mind around was what all the beef and static was about. Why were the Russians the bad guys? What do they think about us? Why does everyone have to go to war simply because the leadership can't seem to agree? I couldn't just settle on the evasive responses given by my teachers. I had a lot of questions, and rather than say, "I don't know," I'd be chastised for disturbing the rest of the class because, apparently, my teachers didn't know and may have been embarrassed by the fact that they couldn't answer certain questions I had, so in turn, I had to be seen as the asshole in this exchange.

From the first grade on through to (12th), every day for (5) days out of a week, we recited the Pledge of Allegiance. I ask, "Why?", and I get a bunch of weird responses, which makes me ask more questions, which only led up to more weird responses that made me ask more questions. Eventually, I learned just to shut up and bear with not knowing "Why?", and accept that this is just the way it is because somebody said so. Either that or continue to be punished due to my ignorance. Man, I hated schooling. I mean, really, how do you not know why schoolchildren are being made to pledge an oath of allegiance to a flag, a symbol? How does an adult let such a question become a point of contention between them and a child? A teacher is a leader of sorts, so we tend to follow their cues when subject to their expertise. If the teacher is found not to be the expert on what they teach, I'm certain that is a problem; so, if this lack of expert knowledge is exposed by a child nonetheless, shit is going to hit the fan. In this case, my social studies teacher would have a fit, which in turn would send me into a fit, but I'm the asshole that caused all of this. I didn't know what was going on. I just received the information from the back end when I got a whipping for being the class clown or throwing temper tantrums. I'm sure that me being disciplined for my outburst in class was satisfying and maybe even gratifying to these good teachers of mine, and because they were the direct source of my pain, I didn't trust them. I didn't like them. I stopped making myself accessible to them. I learned to do a little more than just enough to get by, and that seemed to make everybody happy.

Still, certain questions I had went unanswered so long that I started to really buy into the idea that either I'm not supposed to know or the answers I'm looking for don't exist. The latter of the two has its own severe implications, which suggests that it is absolutely something wrong with me and with my thoughts. If that's the case, how long will it be for the people within a child's social circle to collapse around the idea of her or him having a sociological disorder that has psychological traits, whether such ideas are supported or not? I'm a (70's) baby from the hood. We self-diagnose, so we typically self-medicate, and my medicine of choice at the time came from my ability to conceptualize an alternative reality and produce that world and its cast of characters through drawing.

How emphatic is it that someone can create an entire thing of visual and aesthetic beauty with their ability to manipulate a line? This is what I could escape to and rely on when I needed to get lost and sidestep the bullshit. If there is one drawback to being equipped with this ability, it's that everyone suddenly becomes a critic. Your work stops being yours and becomes the subject of scrutiny. For that reason, it becomes difficult to silence the noise because at the moment you needed that solace and sought out your escape, someone jumped in with the opinions and questions. It becomes invasive. The truth is that I was always an introvert, quiet, soft-spoken, and reserved, which is partially due to the discipline of my parents, so drifting off into drawing something became a perfect means for me to speak without saying a word. None of this dialogue demanded that there be a conversation between myself and anyone else, just a call and response from my mind to my hand and my hand to my canvas. Speaking of which, my canvas could easily become my desk or the blank page at the front and back of a textbook. I'm certain that I left a nice gallery of art for the underclassmen that came to sit at my old desk and had to work from my old books because I always could drift off in classes that couldn't hold my attention or had teachers that weren't quite qualified enough to teach me.

Oddly enough, school was always the top priority when it came to me. Anybody else in my family could drop out, fuck-off, and shuck and jive, but not "your boy." Everybody was on my ass about my grades and my lack of focus, but nobody ever said why. Nobody ever sat me down and explained how vital it is that illiterate, ignorant black boys become educated, functional black men. Nobody ever explained how devastating it is to have an education as a black man or woman in this society. No one ever said that a thorough education is the primary means through which one becomes qualified to perpetuate their existence. Maybe no one in my family ever knew. Regardless, they applied the pressure almost religiously. As I think back, I'm right now trying to rationalize why everyone seemed so interested in what I was doing in school, and I can't come up with much on my own. Still, just from the perspective I have right in this very moment, it could be that because I was the firstborn male of my generation, I inherited the natural obligation to secure and advance the future of my family. I don't know. I wasn't privy to those conversations concerning our family's welfare, but maybe I should have been.

In my youth, I always wanted to work at something or work on something relevant to my taste and enjoyment. I didn't enjoy classwork or homework; I never learned how to study, and I developed a sour taste towards structured learning. Thus, when school was out, I checked all the way out. I was a captive audience of one, from (8:45 AM) until (2:45 - 3 PM). After school was all my time; weekends, holidays, snow days, summer vacation was all me. The year I graduated eighth grade was a rollercoaster ride for me, and it became a summer of revelations that would change the course of my life forever.

Two to three weeks before my graduation, I came home from school and was greeted by my homeboy, who lived next door. We sat in the kitchen, munched on some junk food, and decided our plans for the evening; translation, "Let's go outside." Normally, we leave our respective houses through the back door because we, speaking of my group of friends, hung out primarily in the alley behind our homes. For whatever reason, on this day, we left through the front door. I lived relatively close to the corner of my block on the southern end, so I could immediately assess the whereabouts of my friends by simply looking to the right. None of the *homies* were out on the block, but I noticed two dudes kind of speed walking towards us. The closer they got to us, they seemed to pick up their pace, and you can tell that, at the very least, they had a lot on their minds. I couldn't help now but watch these dudes, and I'm locked in. They're just a couple of houses away, and at this point, me and one of these guys catch eye contact as he reaches down into his *dip.* My mind is saying, "Oh shit!" but I can't fix my mouth to say a word. They cross the steps to the house next door, to my right, and the dude pulls a rolled-up paper bag from his waistband and tosses it towards me. I see the bag as it lands right into the corner of my steps, and then I darted my eyes back in the direction of these two weirdos as they passed us, turned the corner, and took off running. Now I speak the words, "Oh shit!" because seemingly out of nowhere, two patrol cars and two unmarked cars came speeding up the block and screeching their way around the corner. Next, two *Knockas* came flying past us on foot, rounding the corner giving chase, which is the point where my homeboy decided to spectate. As soon as he went to the corner, I turned back to see if anyone else would happen by or was tuned into the events taking place. I waited a couple of seconds, then reached down and grabbed that paper bag. I shoved it in my back pocket, waived for my homeboy to follow me, and we went back into my house, shut and dead-bolted the door, and marched down into the basement.

I can tell that the contents in this bag are loose; nevertheless, I was hoping it was money inside. We got into the basement, and my homeboy has a confused look on his face. You see, he never saw the bag get tossed, so he had no idea while I was calling him away from the excitement outside. He also never saw me pick up the bag, so his already big eyes would like to have jumped out of his head when I pulled the bag from my pocket and emptied its contents onto an old table we used when we had guests at the house. You would have thought we hit the jackpot just based on his expression, but only because whatever this stuff was, it looked like a lot of it. Endless white gel caps came pouring onto the table-top, and he looked at me and asked, "What the fuck is that?" I said, "I don't know." Then he countered, asking me where I got it from, and I explained. He looked at the gel caps, then looked at me and said, I think it's drugs. Now it makes sense. The two dudes obviously at some point realized that the police were on their heels, and so they needed to get rid of their stash somehow before they got caught. Of course, I couldn't put any of this together at the time. I had no clue about anything that goes on in that world. I know what I hear, but I don't understand the language, so we decided to go and talk to one of our older homeboys for some insight. He immediately looked at the stuff and said, "I think it's dope. I'm not (100%) sure, though; let's go ask my mother." We walked up to her room, where she greeted us, and upon seeing this dope, she confirmed that that's what it was, dope or what the rest of the known world calls heroin. Then she hit me with a flurry of questions, "Where did you get this from?" "Who did it belong to?" "You didn't hit somebody's stash, did you?" "Whatchu' gon' do with it?" "Who else knows that you got this shit?" "Did you count it?" After I satisfied her inquiry, she told me to sit down, and she told her son and my other homeboy to "Get out!" We both sat on her bed, and we counted out (350+) gel caps, around (354-356). She told me that they were Dimes, which meant that each cap was worth ten dollars. Then she asked, "Do you know how much money this is worth right now?" I did the math and came with up over ($3500). Then she said, "I could sell it for you if you want, but we gotta' split the cash." Needless to say, I agreed. I mean, what else could I do? I never sold a slice of cake. How else am I supposed to get rid of this stuff?

The next day as I was on my way home from school, walking through their block, my homeboys' mother was sitting out on the steps, smoking a cigarette with another lady. She waved me over, and the other lady left as I approached. Usually, whenever I see her, she always greets me with a smile, but today she has this stern look as we walked into her house. I turned to shut the door behind me, and when I turned back, this good woman was holding the biggest stack of money in my face I'd ever seen in real life. Now she's smiling. I'm smiling. Shit, we're just smiling ear to fuckin' ear. We walked up and into her bedroom, and she said, "Count it out. I don't play no games. This is everything." Once I was done counting, the money was short ($3500) by over ($100). She asked me what I came up with, and I told her. She explained that everyone can't always afford to pay ten dollars, so if they were close to ten, she accepted their short money somewhere no less than seven bucks. "Baby, some of these people need this shit 'cause they ill. You can't be like some of these petty mutha' fuckas' around here chasing every penny. You gotta' be good to the *game* if you want it to be good to you. Besides, this is all profit. All free money." She counted me out ($1750) even, accepting the low end of the split, and then asked me, "Whatchu' think about being my partner?" She told me that she knew some people that would sell her the dope for wholesale at a good price if she spent over ($500) with them, and apparently, this is an opportunity she'd been waiting for.

The deal was that all I had to do was invest some money, and she'd match my investment, buy the product, sell it, and teach me everything I needed to know about the *dope game*. After holding onto that knot and seeing all that money, my answer came without hesitation. We split everything down the middle. I thought for a second about holding onto the thousand and investing the ($750), but if we both put in the thousand, we'd be able to buy more dope, which means we sell more dope, make more money, and have more money to split. Hell, I had that money spent the moment I put it in her hands. As soon as school was out for the summer, class was in session for me. It was only a few days left until graduation, so I knew that I didn't have to go to school until the day of. Every morning I was at my new partner's house, where she'd either cook us breakfast or order us some food from the breakfast spot down the street, a block away. We just talked all morning or watch movies and then talk.

One morning, about a week after graduation, she sent her son, my big homeboy, to my house to get me. I cleaned up, got dressed, and went to her house. I was approaching her door when it opened and she and a man I had never seen before hugged as he left. We walked into the kitchen, and on the table was a sandwich bag that she picked up and tossed to me. "That's (20) grams of raw right there. Ten for you, ten for me." I went to stick my hand in the bag to see what this weird substance would feel like, and she snapped, "Don't touch that shit with your bare hands! That shit will get in your pores. Always put on these gloves when you gotta' handle that shit." She motioned to a box of latex gloves like you see in hospitals. From there, she showed me everything, just as she promised; how to weigh the drugs, how to test the numbers, or in other words, the potency of the dope. She taught me how to cut and what to use to cut the drugs with. The one thing she didn't have to tell me or teach me, the one thing that is the single most important detail that she never said to me outright was never to use the shit. She didn't have to say it, but that lesson is supposed to be (#1) on the bucket list of do's and don'ts. I never tried heroin or cocaine. I was too scared. I grew up seeing the gradual decline of people who got hooked on drugs. I lived with people who fell victim to their addictive personality disorders. All animals are creatures of habit. Our habits are developed out of the need to navigate within our habitat... the place where we develop our habits at. We move in a way that our minds become recorders of our successes and failures; thus, if it's simply a matter of intellect, then in our minds, we must repeat our successes to minimize our propensity to fail. We like stuff that makes us feel good. I believe I can safely say that we immensely enjoy that sensation, and if we could find a way only to feel good, that's all that we'd ever endeavor towards. Now, I said all of that to illustrate that everyone has an addictive personality. The addictive personality, when not held in check, is now a disorder that is manifested in self-debilitating behaviors. To my peers and me, if you use heroin or cocaine, that made you a junky, and that was the source of my fear. I will be remiss if I fail to mention how that standard of being viewed by us as a junky didn't include our family and friends. Yes, they were exempt from that scrutiny, despite their drug habit(s). They were still human to us.

I remind you that I'm, at this time, not even (14) years old. Ever since I can remember, people have told me that I have an old soul. I don't know. Maybe my level of exposure to the streets and street people from that point when I was a (4) year old boy effectively exercised and severed my soul from its childhood tether. Perhaps, that innocence was forever lost to a reality I still can't easily comprehend. In that vein, I was introduced to and given my first opportunity to get high and/or drunk when I was just (9) years old. That was my first-time smoking weed. That was the first memory I had of drinking alcohol. Surely you must know that those first times were followed by many spontaneous excursions that I can't count. No, I wasn't a (9) year-old weed-head or lush. Still, I wasn't bashful when it came time to get faded. I'm thinking about all of this and the fact that I honestly can't tell you what I was supposed to be doing at those various points in my life that I was being exposed to the contributing factors to delinquency. I didn't turn into a child kingpin or some horrible, evil little bastard that terrorized my neighborhood. Instead, I was a shy, quiet kid who had a deep appreciation for pretty girls, music, art, and romance. I hated schooling, but I enjoyed the process of learning if I could learn on my own terms. Begrudgingly, I went through high school and graduated, but those next four years that made up my high school career were absolutely insane for so many reasons. Mainly because life is coming, quick, and is coming in an indiscriminate and unapologetic way. Grown-up decisions have to be made, and eventually, against my own natural inclinations, I have to speak up. Everything I've ever learned at home, at school, and in the streets are going to be tried and tested by everyone, from brief acquaintances and some strangers to the people I loved and trusted the most. But isn't that life? That's how this goes for everyone, including me. I pledge allegiance. I pledge... allegiance. I can't even forget that I pledged my allegiance, my unwavering, undying loyalty to...

Chapter 4
Rights of a Man

If anyone had asked me before July of (2003) how a prisoner can get put out of a prison, I likely would have looked at you like you were crazy for asking me something like that and walked away... On July (5, 2001), I was transferred to the Maryland Correctional Training Center, MCTC, in Hagerstown, Maryland. This was technically my second transfer since leaving Diagnostics, making this my third placement in a prison within (5) years. The first two, (MCI-H and MCI-J), were on a socio-cultural level, polar opposites. Administratively, Hagerstown was run by white people; black people ran Jessup. There can be no mincing of words and no mistaking the fact that you are in prison if you're in Hagerstown or Jessup, but the oppression looks and feels different; which that fact alone is a threatening psychosis that poses a genuine danger to any prisoner, black, white or other. We'll revisit this later...

Coming into the system, an individual has to determine how they will do their respective time. Speaking as an individual who has never been in the system, initially, you were driven by your misconceptions of prison life that were gassed up by media exaggerations and political dramatizations that have enveloped your mind. You believe that, in a nutshell, people who are in prison ceased being human once they come to prison; like they check their humanity at the door and suddenly become these weird animals that are invigorated by their high libidos and ravenous appetites for mayhem and destruction. You tend to fail to consider that these characterizations are an oversimplified subindex idealized as the catalyst for the placement of a person or people in isolation by those authorities who determine the herd's ultimate destiny; until, you become one of us; the isolated.

The ostracized. It doesn't matter the circumstances that brought you here. It only matters that you're here, and since you're here, you fit the bill. It doesn't matter that those hardened criminals became hardened and even more so, that in today's prison system, such people are now in the vast minority, probably the lower (2%), because they have been able to diagnose those particular personalities. That isn't to say that the diagnosis comes intact with a prognosis because the system as it stands is not equipped to function in that capacity. Here's the thing, though... to be housed in any correctional institution, every prisoner must first be processed and assessed in the Diagnostic Classification Center, where you are classified according to your assessed needs, psychologically, intellectually, etc., and then sent to the institution that is equipped to provide for those needs. This process effectively broke down in the mid to late (80s), and by the time I came to prison in the mid (90s), it was completely obsolete. A systematic and cultural overhaul took place wherein the ideal of corrections took on a new complexion, literally. The War on Drugs of the Nixon Era politics started a ripple that gradually grew into a wave by the time Reagan grabbed the baton. It took (6) presidential terms, from Nixon to Clinton, for a theme to take root and the ripple that would become a tidal wave that overwhelmed an entire generation and class of people with the tough on crime politics that spawned the genesis of the Super Predator and Clinton's crack laws. The characterization and dehumanizing politics of population control through the maintenance of neo-slavery and neo-colonialism have overcrowded the entire prison system in the U.S. to almost triple its intended capacity in less than (30) years...and here I am.

On a personal note, I don't know if there is anything I hate more than stereotyping and stigmatizing. For me, that hits on a different level of injustice and disrespect, so naturally, I rebel, as I believe anyone who was subjected to being stereotyped and/or stigmatized should rebel. I believe in the power of our uniqueness and that our individuality should be respected enough to give a person room to excel at what makes them marvelous human beings, being human and humane. Stereotyping is lazy and leaves too much room for error when we find ourselves in a position to make any determination on how we treat other people. We shouldn't shortcut that essential process.

When I, just maybe a few short weeks of coming into city jail, began to make a genuine attempt at processing these charges I'm facing. I felt like my brain was going to explode. I was at my wit's end trying to figure this shit out, the who's, what's, where's, when's, why's and how's. I was exhausted in every way, and I thought that I was suffering from some type of depression, so I submitted a request to speak with the psychiatrist. I've never dealt with depression, and I've certainly never seen a shrink, so I didn't know what to expect or what was going on with me mentally. When I got to the office area, I was (4th) in line out of (6) of us. I sat in the waiting area as the doctor came out and called us one by one. From the first gentleman who walked into the office, no one shut the door behind them, and I was absolutely amazed at what I heard from this doctor. First of all, the fact that the conversation was broadcast to everyone within earshot was enough to sound off alarms in my head. Something's absolutely wrong if a licensed professional blatantly violates his own code of ethics, going as far as to make these conversations public, when he simply could have instructed any of us to shut the door. The first man stepped in, took his seat, and the dialogue went like this, I'll paraphrase...

"Good afternoon. You put in a request to see me. What do you want to talk about?"

"How are you doing, Sir? I came to see you 'cause ever since I got locked-up, I have just been going through some things. I can't sleep, and I can hardly eat. Plus, I've been having problems talking to my family."

"How long have you been locked up?"

"About (3) weeks."

"Have you been arrested before?"

"Yes. This is the third time."

"For how long?"

"The first time, I was over here for 'bout (6) months, then for 'bout a year."

"Now, you're back on a new charge?"

"Yeah."

"Do you use drugs?"

"Yes, Sir."

"Are you on drugs right now?"

"Huh? Like is I'm high right now?"

"Yes."

"No. I'm not high."

"What drugs do you use?"

"Heroin."

"Do you use crack?"

"No, Sir."

"You don't smoke crack?"

"No, Sir."

"What were you arrested for?"

"C.D.S. possession and armed robbery."

"Do you feel depressed?"

"Yeah. I feel like I can't cope. Like, I can't do nothing right, so I don't know, I just get high."

"Do you feel like you want to hurt yourself? Like, you don't want to live any longer, sometimes?"

"Sometimes."

"So, to me, it's not very difficult to understand what's going on with you. You are a repeat offender and a drug addict who has made one bad decision after the next. Obviously, your family has turned their backs on you because they don't want to keep going down this road with you, right? Why do you think you're here for what, the third time?"

"Huh? I mean, it's like you said, "I be making bad decisions.""

"People who make bad decisions over and over again aren't smart people, would you agree?"

"I mean, I guess so."

"So, you've made more than one decision to come back to jail, right?"

"Yes, Sir."

"So, basically, you are here right now because you're stupid."

"Huh?"

"You're locked up again; this is your third time because you're stupid."

"You know what? I get it now. You saying, like, 'cause I be making stupid decisions, right? So, yeah. If I'm making stupid decisions, then I must be stupid. I get it."

"Because you're stupid."

"Uh-huh, right."

The same dialogue went on with all three of the men sitting in front of me. I couldn't believe this shit. I thought one of them dudes would have strangled this fraud for playing with their intelligence, but instead, they all ate that shit up with a smile. In my mind, I'm thinking that this so-called doctor is getting off on running this weird game on us. It was the same dialogue with the same responses, and I'm genuinely starting to think that somebody is playing a joke on me. My turn... I went through all the preliminaries; why I came to see him, how I was feeling, the charges I was facing, the fact that I'm a new father, the whole nine. I swear, after sitting in that waiting room and listening to this little balding white guy get off for over an hour, I heard him literally turning the conversation into his segue about how he'll convince me that the only thing that's wrong with me is that I'm stupid. I cut him off immediately.

"Listen, man. I heard what you told them guys that came in here before me. Don't try me on that. I came up here to unload and get some feedback on how to calm my thoughts and get myself ready to fight this case. I'm not stupid. Don't call me stupid. Don't try to imply that I'm stupid. Either speak to me with some respect like I'm respecting you, or we don't got nothin' else to talk about."

He paused and sat back in his chair and just stared at me for about (30) seconds. I started to get up to leave, and he said, "What makes you any different than anybody else in this jail?" I told him, "Nothing." He asked me to sit back down, and we began to talk. We didn't talk about me, my case, or my state of mind; we talked about life. Before I knew it, the officer at the desk came in and said it was time for the count and that I needed to leave before the shift changed. He never even got to speak to the last two men that day.

Life is already categorical, but within each category exists an element that simply doesn't fall within the norm. We can all seem the same on the surface but have contextual differences that are just as significant as the things we see about us that look the same. Skin complexion, for example, is like a person's fingerprint; as similar as two skin tones may look, no two are the same. If only in that fine detail exists the uniqueness, how can we possibly prejudge justifiably a person, or people, especially based on beliefs? Beliefs change all the time for a multitude of reasons. Sometimes our beliefs change when challenged with evidence supporting an opposing belief and/or fact. Now, that said, I've done my fair share of stupid things, like anyone else... like everyone else, why would that be the thing, amongst all my other outstanding qualities, that defines me? My situation notwithstanding, I came to prison not knowing who and what I am. I could have become a gambler, a gangster, a bootlicker, a snitch, a dope-fiend, a stick-up kid, a thief;... instead, I became studious, disciplined, audacious, flexible, objective, a philosopher, a builder of institutions, a rebel, on my journey into manhood. The fact of the matter is that my journey has taken me through arduous and dangerous terrain. My journey is peculiar yet not uncommon. I was ill-prepared for the trip, but I learned to equip myself along the way.

By October of (2001), I had been introduced to books such as "Seize the Time" by Bobby Seale, "Enemies" by Dr. Haki Madhubuti, "The Psychopathic Racial Personality" by Dr. Bobby E. Wright, the entire Dr. Naim Akbar collection, "I Write What I like" by Steve Biko, ... I can go on and on. Actually, my introduction to these books came from a most unlikely source; one of my best friends had moved into the cage with me, and every week he could go to his religious service and bring back a different book. The back story to this is that we grew up around each other but never hung out much until after I caught my last charges, and we both were in city jail fighting our cases. We got tight during that year, so after I got found guilty and wound up in the ol' jail (MCI-H), I wrote him and the few good men I knew who were still in the city, basically telling them about my good news. Yeah, I found my path to self-discovery. I'm building with the Nation of Gods and Earths, and I realize that this is what we've been missing; that life-changing spark that will devastate and totally shock us into a new way of thinking. Not long after, he came into the ol' jail and moved on to the tier I was on. He started building with us, but we were both still thuggin' and druggin', which is a sign of youthful uncertainty. You see, at that point in life, I'm (22) years old and one whole year into a cucumber fresh life bid. In my mind, the life-changing, devastation, and shock of being buried alive still haven't resonated. It still hasn't become my reality, so in my mind, I still have one sure foot out of the grave.

I got transferred to (MCI-J) in December (1998), once again leaving my homeboy. He wound up going home but came back in July (2001). On the same day, I got packed up to transfer from (MCI-J) to (MCTC). Just a couple of short months later, word got to me that he was in the jail, so I paid the clerk to have him move into my housing unit. Meanwhile, ever since my arrival in this jail, Intel had been fuckin' with me. I'm not, nor have I ever been in a gang, but a Lieutenant from the Intelligence Unit called me to his office, not (24) hours after my arrival, telling me that I've been validated as a gang member. They took pictures of me and my tattoos, none of which are symbolic of any affiliation, and to make matters worse, this so-called validation of gang affiliation didn't have me affiliated with any particular gang. Yeah, me, coming in at about (160) pounds, "the one-man gang," really?! I remind you that I am studying, still growing up, and trying to find my way, but I'm still uncertain and holding onto my doubtfulness about who I am and who and what I want to become, so I'm still on my bullshit, thuggin' and druggin' part-time. I got the homie moved into the cage with me. We know each other, trust each other and consider one another friends, even more so, brothers. We are on the same shit, so when I finally notice that this mu' fucka' was reading real books and asking me to help him with book reports, it drew me in.

I started asking him questions, which led up to me reading his books when he was chilling, and then later, he just started bringing back two copies of every book he was reading for that week so I couldn't bogart his time with the books. One day we got into a debate over what is probably to this very day one of the most difficult books I've ever read, George Jackson's perennial thesis "Blood In My Eye". It was during that spirited debate that bro' decided to invite me to the service he attended. I went against my personal sense of distrust of dogmatic tenants and religiosity, I went, and upon walking in the doors, I felt a sense of warmth and brotherhood I had never experienced before. I was surrounded by young men, some of who was still teenagers, but you couldn't tell by how they looked. They were mature in ways that I still needed work, but nothing could prepare me for the first message I received that night. They lit a fire up under me, and from that point, I became different. I dug deeper and kept digging. These brothers didn't give me religion, but they gave me something to believe in. They challenged me to challenge myself, figure out who I am, where I came from, my purpose, and how to reach the point where I can define my own reality and create my own destiny.

It became popular around the jail for those serious about learning to build study groups on our respective tiers. Everybody was welcome to sit at our table and break bread, so as our table began to grow, so did people's interest in what we were doing at the table. My homeboy got sent to Patuxent Institution in (2002), per court order, to serve his time in the youthful offender's program. By that time, our study group grew from (6) studious young men to take up the entire bottom tier Rec-Hall for (3) to (4) nights a week. One of the brothers at the table named our study group, "Challenge", a moniker he gave us due to the debates that cropped up regularly, as well as the challenges some of us older gentlemen that were over (25) years old had to face in representing righteousness and propriety to the younger men in our midst. They made us accountable for what we say and do. I loved it, and out of that love was born the fruits of our tremendous hardships; in me was a revolutionary enthusiasm. My focus became developing the institution of manhood, fleshing out these venerable attributes, and remaining steadfast in the face of adversity. Adversity ...

...Do not think for one second that this new undertaking didn't come paired with obstacles. Reading books, studying and having candid discussions, using the dictionary to help expand our vocabulary, and learning how to maximize our use of time and space didn't suddenly create a utopian existence. We were still prisoners. We were still subjected to prison politics, wherein each of us had to become well versed in the language, the lore, and the politicians because we were ushering in a new culture on our tier that started to affect the culture in the entire housing unit. This housing unit has had a reputation for being the most violent, the most dangerous unit on the compound. We called it The Dome or The Danger Zone. It earned its reputation honestly. In situations of confinement, violence is a tool that effectively maintains the checks and balances on both sides of the line. The mere understanding that certain miscalculated actions carry with them violence as a consequence keeps prisoners and prison personnel from being unprofessional. If professionalism is the order of the day, then there is an expectation of appropriateness and how we interact. It's an unspoken contract. There is no need for a handshake, signature, or even a nod; once you enter the arena, you go to work at doing your job, not doing my job or nobody else's, be the best you that you can be, and all will be fine. Once that contract becomes void, it is what it is; chances are the consequences will be harsh enough to effectively eliminate you from the equation. The reason for this is so that everyone has a clear notion of how to navigate successfully within this terrain, and we all need that courtesy, prisoner, and prison personnel alike. Without that, chaos ensues, and the system as a whole shuts down. Do you understand? It's the law and order of things; without law, there can be no order, and nobody wants that.

Before I go on, let me say this, I do not advocate for or promote violence. Violence is a reality, and it does exactly what I said it does in a society. It functions in a way that lets people understand that actions draw out a response. Some responses may indeed be physical and absolutely dangerous, no matter how many people frown upon it. You lessen the propensity of receiving a violent response to your behavior by making a conscious effort toward maintaining professionalism and appropriateness. With that in mind, Challenge is a real thing at this point, and it is changing the scope and how we view ourselves and one another in this environment. Some people don't want a cultural shift in the social dynamic here, speaking directly about the politicians who induced and become the proprietors of the thuggish intolerance and gangsterism in the environments. I would soon learn that the *game* is played on both sides of the line. No one is exempt.

By March (2003), the violence in the jail is at its apex. Prisoners are assaulting one another; officers are assaulting prisoners, and the prisoners have started randomly assaulting officers. Some of these assaults are purely retaliatory stemming from a prisoner being beaten by officers. Some of these incidents were well thought out and executed according to carefully considered planning. We were constantly being locked down, and groups of people were placed in segregation, just because. Our housing unit was at one point being escorted to and from the dining hall by officers armed with teargas guns, suited up in riot gear. We were subjected to strip searches on the compound, outside, on the walk to and from the dining hall. The concentration camp concept was our day-to-day reality. It was at this point that I had been elected to try and present Challenge to the Warden as a means through which to show the administration that some of us are actually making a genuine effort towards excellence despite our current circumstances and to ask that other alternatives to the situations we're collectively dealing with be explored as opposed to locking everyone down or locking people up. Many of the men were suffering, and all of us were being punished for the actions of a few, even after the actual culprits were dealt with. We would get locked down if an officer or officers beat on a prisoner, so the tension and anxieties were constantly turned up. No one knew what to expect on any given day, so I spoke to the Warden, who told me to write him a proposal explaining Challenge to him. I've never written a proposal for anything before, so the proposal turned out to be an elaborate letter asking for permission to open up Challenge to the entire housing unit as a program. Upon receiving the letter, the Warden came to me personally with his response ... "What do you need from me to get this done?", ...

I'm not sure how many of us are cultivated with a trusting nature versus being skeptical. I'm one who takes a person at their word because I was taught that your word is all you have in this world. If you commit to something or someone, the expectation is that you see that all the way through until the end. Some of us committed ourselves to endeavors without doing our due diligence, without utilizing vision, judiciousness, or calmness of thought. As a practice, such ignorance is simply impractical and doesn't normally lead to much more than a hard lesson on the consequences that come as a result of our foolishness. Just as many lives are lost as those that are born due to our lack of understanding the intricacies of commitment; thus, because I am the embodiment of the varying degrees of this misunderstanding, once I commit myself to something or someone, I'm all in, oftentimes to my own detriment. Some people are, in fact, skeptical of me and my intentions; not based on our shared history, because my track record, although not flawless, is impeccable; however, I'm sure many of us have suffered unwarranted, sometimes relentless scrutiny because of someone else's misdeeds and miscalculations. It's not fair, it's certainly not ideal, but people have handled and mishandled people in this way since times immemorial. I've expressed my feelings on this, so how do I explain being placed on administrative segregation, pending transfer, (2) weeks before Challenge as a full-fledged program being opened up to the entire population at (MCTC)?

For years I felt betrayed by the (MCTC) staff and administration because I was dealt with in a way as if I had done something so appalling, reprehensive, and wrong. I sat on segregation for (6) months, in my mind, for nothing. I didn't break any rules, defy institutional policy, nothing. Every (30) days, I had to go for Segregation Review (Seg. Review), where a hearing officer would decide whether to place you back in the general population or not. I didn't see a hearing officer, my Seg. Reviews were conducted by the Gang Task Force, an outside entity that worked with the D.O.C. My first review was conducted by a middle-aged white dude, tall, balding, authoritative voice, kind of husky but one burger away from being considered obese. I sat down, and he asked me what I was doing sitting in front of him. I told him, "I just followed instructions. The man brought me in here and told me to sit in this chair." He looked me over and then looked down into a file folder and said, "Apparently, you're not going to be here much longer. The Captain says she wants you out of this institution. What did you do?" I said, "Sir, I honestly don't know how to answer that question. You got a file in your hand with my name in it, that I'm sure has something written down, accusing me of some egregious act. The Captain wants me out; I don't know why, but you do because it says so right there." He didn't look up from the folder in his hand. He was quiet for a moment, and then he asked, "Do you know who I am?" to which I said, "No, Sir." "I work with the Division of Corrections on a task force that monitors gang activity. It is my job to identify members of Security Threat Groups, facilitate the process of renouncement of one's affiliation, maintain the database that tracks the progression of the Security Threat Groups in and out of prison, and conduct these interviews with validated Security Threat Group members, which has placed you and me in the unique situation we're in today. You've been validated as a member, and quite possibly, a leader, of an STG. But as I'm sitting here, I'm having the damnedest time trying to figure out something... What gang are you apart of, Mr. Shannon? This file has nothing in it."

"Sir, I am not, nor have I ever been in a gang."

"So, how did you get validated?"

"No disrespect, Sir, but how should I know? When I arrived here from (MCI-J) in (2001), a Lieutenant called me into his office, told me that I was 'validated' and that he had to take pictures of my tattoos. That's all I know."

We looked at one another for a few seconds then he asked to see my tattoos. I complied, and to that, he said, "This is bullshit. These aren't gang tattoos. I came here from the West Coast, and I've been in this field for almost (20) years. You have to excuse me, but it pisses me off every time I see this. This file has no listed affiliations, no listed activity, nothing. You're not a gang member. I believe that. You may be an asshole, I don't know, maybe not, but being an asshole doesn't validate someone as a gang member."

In some strange way, I felt a relief come over me as I've never felt before. It was like, "Finally!" Finally, someone is hearing and listening to me. Finally, the record is reflecting the truth about who I believe I am. Finally, I don't have that lingering burden of trying to prove that the work I'm putting in is genuine, meaningful, and love inspired. Someone can see the truth now. I'm moving in the right direction. From July until December, I went for Seg. Review, looking forward to a conversation with this gentleman, who told me that even though he didn't need to see me anymore, he'd still called me out, just to give me an hour or so out of that cell. We just talked like old friends, and when December came, he called me in to say goodbye and wish me well into my fight for freedom. He shook my hand and seemed happy for me. We were not friends; we both knew that. We both knew that we each represented opposing philosophies and worldviews, but what we shared was mutual respect as opponents in a convoluted, intricate, and diabolical game of what he once described to me as Cops and Robbers. My perspective differed, then and now, but that's life, an entanglement of principles and feuding perspectives. There's an eventuality that comes from all of this, where throughout our plight, many good soldiers fall victim to inconsistency, pride, and doubt... We will determine that our youthful impetuousness and ravenous appetite for foolishness is not the sin, but that the sin is in our utter wastefulness of the borrowed time we have and the total lack of respect for the distinguishment of our brethren. I've always believed in my personal vibrance, even in those moments in my life where someone has intentionally tried to make my world dim, dull, and void of color. I've only just begun to realize, if only in these last few seconds, that as individuals, we all possess that warm glow, that thing that attracts the external energies, the spirits of good and evil. As such, in some way, we all want to be seen, recognized, and or/or understood. As a vessel, we all need to know that we carry within us precious cargo, which is a commodity that makes us valuable. Ignorance and a lack of human sensitivity stymie our ability to see value in integrity, intelligence, patience, and peace of mind, body, and spirit. Ignorance makes one abusive, callous, and mean; it makes one miserable, and misery makes one weak. I refuse to be that guy, especially since I'm being made the subject of that guy's insecurities and lack of balance and harmony. In fact, if I'm honest, I've come to enjoy ruining that guy's day when I greet him with a loud, proud, "Top of the morning, Sir!" and every morning is nevertheless the same. Right after I put that guy on point, I immediately pray for peace, continued prosperity and paradise, because I've learned that everything I say and do, is received by that guy as a sign of aggression, a war cry, if you will. I pray for forgiveness for my indecorousness and shameless manipulation of diction. I pray that my vehemence is insightful and that my determination is rewarded with depth, vision, and fortitude. I pray for shelter from the wrath of unvetted charlatans who campaign in silence for my doom, death, and destruction. I pray for life and liberation, justice to be just, and the ability to revolutionize, redefine, and reinstate our gloriousness... I feel the glow and the radiance and the heat of the eventualities that ought to be because of our inevitable interaction, but I haven't even begun to shine...

Chapter 5
Conspiratorial Interest

Looking back on my youth as I slow-walked my way into that drug culture, that underworld, I don't know if there's anything a person could say or do to prepare themselves or someone else for what they're about to see. My first day as a so-called Dope-boy began with one of the most frightening experiences of my life. The night before, I stayed over at a friend's house to get up early enough to meet up with the homie that was giving us the work. We got up at around six in the morning, freshened up, grabbed a (7-11) breakfast (donuts and soda), then went to meet up with dude. He showed us too large zip lock bags stuffed with gel caps of heroin, tucked them in a duffel bag, and we started walking. We were (5) blocks away from where the shop was set up, which is about a (7 to 10) minute walk, and it's a straight shot from where we started. I could see the people out and about, you know, the typical foot traffic and activity one would expect at (7:00) AM on a summer day. We crossed the first street, and as soon as we stepped into that block, what looked to me like maybe (10 to 15) people, chillin', talkin' shit, dumping their garbage, having a smoke or sweeping up trash, suddenly grew to what looks like (40 to 50) people. They came from inside their houses, from alleyways, from out of nowhere, but what's more, everything they were doing stopped. The entire block froze, the people stopped talking, stopped moving, and all I could hear now was the traffic behind us. They were watching us. Silent eyes bearing down on us, ripping at my flesh, daring me to flinch, begging me to surrender something. Anything. When we got to the middle of the block, the big homie yelled out, (9) o'clock! That break in the silence startled the shit out of me! What's worse is that the same thing happened on every block we went through. Every block. The silence. The eyes. They see, and they know. I wanted to run, but it was like I couldn't get up the courage to haul ass out of there. It felt like my feet were dug in ankle-deep in the concrete. I've never seen anything or felt anything like this in my young life. When we reached our destination, I finally decided to look back, and maybe I was trippin', but it seemed like most of those people were gone.

I asked the dudes I was with why all of that just happened; why did all those people seem to pop up? Why they suddenly got so quiet, and why in the fuck were they staring at us? The big homie said it plain, with this slight grin on his face and his already large eyes exploding out of his head, "They was waiting for us." I didn't even want him to elaborate because I had a slight notion about where I had found myself, so I knew I couldn't let anybody know how green I was, or I'd be food. I did everything I could to try and calm my breathing and my thoughts while I received our instructions on how the day's operations are supposed to go, but I couldn't get the butterflies out of my stomach.

"Shop opens from (9:00 AM till 9:00 PM); two people in the house, no music, no TV, no sleeping; only one person comes to this house to get pills, only one person comes to this house with money; keep the house clean; if you get a page, code (911), dump the pills in this bucket of acid and chill until you get the next page, code (60); hitters take no shorts, no change and check all bills; "O is my Lieutenant, do what he says, it's just that simple."

What? Lieutenant? What, me? I was blown away. The two dudes who were to be in the stash house started counting out each pill to be sold, and the big homie pulled me to the side. "Listen, I need you to handle this shit and handle these niggas. I know you fresh, but you got it. You my second in command out here 'cause I like how you carry yourself. I chose you 'cause you got what I need, so let's get some money."

I wasn't even old enough at (15) to have an ego, so because I was so anxious, it felt to me like *game*. Knowing what I know now, that's the nature of the beast, ... find out what they like and give 'em so much that they think they're on top of the world but give them just enough so that they'll keep coming back. I've never been one who needs compliments heaped on me, but if I do a good job at something, I think everyone enjoys an 'attaboy from time to time, and I'm no different in that respect. I was out there for the money, period, not because I had ego maniacal aspirations, so yeah, let's get some money.

It was a long day of revelations and more anxiety. The foot traffic is crazy, and my head is constantly on a swivel. For all intents and purposes, the block is mine. I'm running the show, and I don't have a fuckin' clue about what I'm doing. Any questions, "Ask O," the answer is always, "No." The poor runners would have all died of heatstroke waiting on me to permit them to stop the "Mr. Softee-Truck." Throughout the day, I'm seeing people who I would never have thought use drugs, some of my friends' parents, a few of my classmates, people. Real people. Before that day, I could only assume that people who got high were junkies and that junkies weren't human, didn't have families and or people who loved them; they had no identity, so they were easy for me to see but not see. Now, I noticed them. I'm beginning to see them, but I still couldn't recognize nor comprehend what I was looking at. What's worse is that the more I'm seeing these people, the less empathy I have for their state of being, the less respect I have for them. Many of them are making complete fools of themselves; they're stealing from themselves, the women are allowing themselves to become pincushions, for a pill. It's sick ... No, really, it's sick... No, listen to me, they're literally sick ...

...It took me many years to understand that. Now, right now, as you're following this, ask yourself, "How long do you think it took for me to realize how sick I was?" You see, that's part of it, part of that thing that feeds the beast. At the point where you allow yourself to believe that you can move within this world that's disease-ridden and not somehow become infected, you are really tripping'. No one in that world comes out of it unscathed, but not just anyone who wanders into that world can survive the onslaught of bright ideas that swirl about in a vicious cycle of cat and mouse. In fact, the chances of survival are slim at best. But here I am, a scrawny little mutha' fucka 'surrounded by some serious heavyweights, who trivialized my sense of direction and are hell-bent on securing my soul to replenish their reservoir, 'cause they're batteries are low, and their tanks are on *E* and a half, so they are running on fumes and desperate for a win. The question becomes, ... "Which vessel has the allure, the perfect pitch to persuade me to dive head-first in their direction?", Me, the young blood. Imagine that. Imagine, if you will, those of you that know me now, me in some *abandominium*, in a dark corner, trying to shove a needle in what may be the last good vein I had left; imagine me in a ski mask, pushing the barrel of an old, rusted gun to somebody's grandma demanding money? Imagine me the good brother you know and love, in that same *abandominium* with your mother or your sister, making her do unimaginable acts with me and all of my homeboys for a lousy ($10) hit; imagine me, in a covert position, pointing out other dudes in the *game* to detectives and watching him get arrested based on my information; imagine me, me convincing a child that they could be a part of that world, that underworld and get rich ... These are the thoughts of one who became a member of a dead class of people and is looking towards an end. You see, there is a way to become a survivor in the final analysis, but one has to come to grips with the full scope of what they were doing while they were fully engaged in the war. You have to realize the depths of your individual role and fully comprehend your participation to reach a point of reconciliation between you, your soul, and the souls of those lost due to your youthful indiscretions and lack of attentiveness to detail. I'm at a point now where I find myself mentally, emotionally, and spiritually out of the *game* but still suffering the ramifications of my childish pursuits in being physically trapped by the mutha' fucka' that gave us the *game*. Now what?

Now comes clarity. The more time I spent out there hustlin', the more of the people's pain I began to feel, the more of a stand-up dude I tried to be, despite the realities of the immediate contradictions that always conveniently become apparent. Looking back, I was a blue-collar hustler, the relatable, reliable type, self-made, diligent, quiet, intense, and focused. I earned it because I handled my own work, and I was always on the clock. If somebody worked for me, they worked with me, and they were always addicts. For me, the benefits of working with addicts far outweigh the shortcomings. I was raised in the streets by some cruddy mutha' fuckas' who balanced out their bullshit by teaching me the principles they wanted me to apply when it came time for me to realize how cruddy they were if the time came for me to call them on their shit. I say this to say I could be a cruddy mutha' fucka' from moment to moment, and there was a point that I would argue that those were some of my best moments in the streets. I was my most innovative self, creating new ways to maximize my input and minimize my output. I knew what I was capable of because I had been tried and tested, my ideas went through the natural progression of trial and error, so I didn't cultivate anyone who had my same hunger at any point in time. An addict had a whole different system of ideals, so I felt like I could predict their moves because I had my thumb on the pulse of their motivations and aspirations. Someone like me could be ferocious when their eyes grow to the size of their belly. That type of shit won't be denied when that time comes. There may not be any surviving that. On the other hand, I've had addicts who've stolen from me. They may have caught me on a good night, the money was good, the weed was dank, the liquor was wet, and, in their slickness, they made off with a few pills, right under my nose. The problem is, I can count, and I constantly count, so even if I didn't see it, I know it happened, but I already accounted for the loss of a few pills before I even hit the block. The way I see it, this mutha' fucka' just helped me make (3, 4, 5) thousand dollars today, and this idiot just cuffed ($20) worth of drugs. Damn, "You's a slick mutha' fucka'. My objective wasn't to take advantage of their illness, like out of being cruddy and cheap, understand this, ...these people are everywhere, they know everybody, and they see and hear everything, so if they're on the team, they keep me informed and sensitive to my surroundings. They are the streets. If they'd only ask, I'd give them whatever they want, money, food, clothes, cigarettes, drugs, whatever. They were invaluable to me, so I had to show how valuable I could be to them. They'd be the ones who'd protect me by keeping me aware.

Do me a favor, and you do the math. I've never been robbed, never even been on that radar; not for nothing but, what would a stick-up kid want with a blue-collar nigga like me? We're both in the basement, trying to find our way to the ground floor. Truth be told, for me, that wasn't even camouflaged; that's how I lived. What you see is what you get, so you saw me drinking Richards with a fug and a blunt, eating Cup-of-Soups and Egg-Foo Yung sandwiches. I rode mountain bikes. I paid *Boosters* for clothes, appliances, and any random assortment of materials. I was grimy and hogged the corner like a street sign. I was never obnoxious and loud. I was calm, quiet, and patient. My presence was disarming and didn't alert trouble, as I was determined not to be the *lick*. Man, I thought that if you "be good to the *game*, the *game* would be good to you," as the saying goes, so I tried to apply my sense of high moral rectitude to everything I did in the streets ...Oh, how noble for a dude who sells narcotics for a living. But we often excel at living out our contradictions, even if we don't believe that we do. To me, high moral rectitude simply meant, don't snitch, don't go against the grain; just do the kind of shit and be the kind of person to people that keeps your dignity, respect, and integrity intact. Still to this day, my good name remains untarnished, and I'm proud of that, but in the final analysis, what good did it do me? Let's see...

...I came up around guys that were tight-knit and represented one another accordingly. We never had gangs back then; it was more about protecting and holding down the fort, wherever that may be. By the time the drug culture seeped into our neighborhoods, we had firmly established our bonds and friendships, started puberty, and our desires matured with our worldview. I became more aware of our economic station because the things I wanted and the activities I pursued now have a price tag that, although not astronomical, was a point of contention as the conversation was now about bills. I hated asking for things, so much so that I did whatever I could to try and avoid that uncomfortable conversation. I wasn't old enough to get a job, so I would save up my lunch money, which came to a total of ($7.50) if I held on for the entire week. That was just enough for some fast food, way before the dollar menu. I got creative. I figured out that I could go to the market and buy ($3) worth of ground beef, a dollar worth of cheese, and a bag of hamburger rolls, which was about ($1.25) I'd make about (5-6) big house burgers and sell them for ($2) a sandwich. Quick flip, I doubled my money, and now I can chip in on a pizza with the *homies* or have enough to go to the movies. I couldn't do that all the time, though, because shit was happening outside that I just couldn't stand to miss out on. Girls, parties, parties, girls, girls, girls, and girls. You had to be able to dress, which for us kids meant we needed designer gear; in other words, the shit that Mama couldn't afford until it was out of fashion. My lunch money wasn't going to cut it, and neither was slingin' house burgers. So, on a fateful day in East Baltimore, a (13) year old boy is presented with an option, pick up that brown paper bag and throw it away with the rest of the garbage, or take that bag and its contents to someone who can transform this boy and his world, forever.

We got money in the streets with who we grew up with; the same circle whom we fought for, broke bread with, shared realities, and bled and shed blood for. Every friend was your best friend, and your best friend was your brother. On one hand, I can count how many of us are still alive, not in prison or strung out on drugs. In the final analysis, my friends, my brothers killed one another off. Literally. I, not for lack of good fortune, wasn't around to see the evil we pursued that left (97%) of my circle extinct. Best friends are slaughtered at the hands of the people they trust, not for the typical bullshit, money, status, women, or materialism, but for the *game*. The allure of the streets turned suckers into savages, and the strongest of the strong got caught in a tangled web of cold steel and concrete. At one time, it was simple; life was filled with dreams of finding my candy girl and summer madness. We built clubhouses out of milk crates and plywood, rode our bikes down cannonball hill, and climbed rooftops that seemed like we were on top of the world. I love being up on the roof. I can see clear across the East Baltimore skyline. I shied away from going to the edge, but even on the rare occasion where I'd venture close enough, I never looked down; I always looked outward to the horizon.

I traded in my zip lock bags of penny candy, *Superbubbles*, and *Blow Pops* for tiny vials of cocaine and bundles of heroin. The last time I saw the East Baltimore skyline, I was looking from my cell window, on the (6th) floor of the Maryland Diagnostic Classification Center in December (1996). Long gone were those days of carelessness. I'm a number amongst a mass count that makes me one of the declassified. I'm locked up, locked away, and locked out. For upwards of (18) hours a day, I'm locked in, locked in with my memories, emotionalism, mania, demons, and cage-mate. What's crazy is that, despite my circumstances, my sense of urgency came from the idea that I could sell some smack to pay for a lawyer to give my time back on appeal. That bright idea came from that guy. He was a dope-fiend, a former boxer turned pimp, that in his own way showed me another side of the *dope game*. I've sold dope on and off since I was (13) years old, and now I'm (21). This man was somewhere in his late ('50s) doing his (4th) bid, and according to his testimony, he'd been sniffing heroin since he was (16). I thought I knew something about smack, but this man was some sort of an expert. "See, Young-Blood, it's a numbers game. If you can't count, you can't win!" We talked about politics, history, his criminal career, and drugs. We read a magazine article that talked about trafficking heroin from Malaysia, Nigeria, and Afghanistan to New York, Baltimore, and California. "Do you know what you was selling youngin'? You was selling (98%) cut.

That shit wasn't dope." The way he broke the situation down was basically that the government-controlled the flow of narcotics; the purity of the heroin was contingent on how many shipments of the drug got seized and how much was allowed through during DEA raids on borders and ports.

"If they knocked off (200) tons of heroin, best believe (100 to 200) tons made it through."

"How do you know?"

"Think about it. The US government has the most advanced intelligence in the world. How the fuck is (100) tons of anything coming in this mutha' fucka', and they don't know it? They've been pushin' dope for years. They needed a way to control us, 'cause once we wake up, they know all of this American dream shit is over."

"Why you get high then? If you know you bein' controlled? Why you fuck with that shit?"

"Shorty, I'm sick."

In my best state of mind, all I can think about what he's telling me is that it's no way possible he could know any of this shit. He's on some conspiracy shit, trying to make an excuse for being strung out. That's all I need right now, an old dope-fiend, fiendin' out on me like he's some kind of a crusader, as if I don't have enough problems of my own with the government, now I got this old nigga in my ear seeking some sort of recompense on Uncle Sam for the hole in the septum.

"Slim, you sold smack, but you got in the *game* when all of the dope was garbage. Shit, the best dope in Baltimore right now is maybe (1 ½ two 2%) raw. Any dope in the city that's (3%) raw is killing people, so unless the niggas out there want to get indicted for a bunch of fatal overdoses, they cut the dope to death."

Now I'm listening...

...East Baltimore, when I was a kid, still on the steps, naive to the realities of the struggle, was a fascinating place to me. The people had a vibe that I could easily be in tuned with, which has always been important to me. When I became aware of the darkness that envelops my side of town, it strangely moved me. At once, it seemed like everybody was on drugs. I'm beginning to notice things about my neighborhood and its groovy citizens; from one corner to the next is dope. In between the lines are us, the people, the pollution, the rodents, and the *abandominiums*. Block after block, for a quarter of a mile; it's an open-air drug market; around the corner and down the street is the start or the end of a whole 'nother dope strip that runs for a quarter of a mile. We can do this all day, meaning that I could name streets and areas across the city map where heroin is sold and if we just stay within a (10) block radius, I can show you (5 to 7) holes. I'm sitting here, right at this moment, wondering if I ever considered back then how economically destitute we were. We were poor. Being poor made us inventive and strangely considerate, so we moved with a peculiar rhythm, that vibe; I was keen to it. I've been on strips that may have five different shops, selling smack from the same plug, that's cut five different ways, and everybody is selling anywhere between (10 to 30) thousand dollars' worth of heroin a day. So, it seems that poor people don't suffer enough of being addicted to heroin for it to be considered a crisis. Thus, poor people, my people, don't get the same crisis prevention measures and media exposure as does the affluent dealing with an opioid epidemic. What am I missing? Heroin isn't an opioid because the opioid is synthetic and only has the characteristics of opiate narcotics such as heroin. We couldn't afford opioids where I'm pushin'.

Bearing that in mind, (2%) raw seems palatable now, considering. We couldn't afford better. You have to wonder, though, from (10 to 30,000) a day is a lot of dimes. Who is buying (3000) pills? If I sold pills for ($1), I could make a professional's yearly salary in (10) days on the lowest end. In one month at ($1) a pill and a (3000) pill cut off, I could make corporate American money, ... ($90,000); in one year, that's over a million bucks. We sold ($10) pills. I never seen that kind of money or even counted money that way in my head, but besides all of that, where is all this money coming from? Where is it going? Who is it going to? I want you to picture this ($30,000) going to just one out of (5) shops, where the laziest click is taking in ($10,000) on the same day. We get a war, while on the other hand, they get an epidemic. We get (98%) of additives that range from coffee grounds to baby laxatives, while the other (2%) is waiting to get cut at least six more times, leaving a heroin addict with just (0.1666666%) of the actual drug, in which a dope-fiend considered to be a missile or the best of the best. Do you understand? Have you ever really done the math? It's all addition through division. If I buy (1) gram of heroin that's at standard (1 ½%) raw, I'll pay ($100 to $150); I can probably cut, divide, that gram at (6) to (1), or (6) grams of cut to one gram of heroin and make ($600 to $700) off of the one. True, I made more than one gram of heroin when I cut it, which automatically suggests that the dope was multiplied, but the reality is that the dope was actually divided up amongst 6 grams of cut. The dope didn't gain potency, the cut did, and we don't advertise that we're selling B&Q (which is a mixture of mannitol and quinine used commonly as Cut); we say we're selling dope, smack, heroin. That's like Kellogg's or General Mills telling you they're selling you a box of sugar. No, it's cereal, they say.

Nobody I knew in the streets thought about drugs this way, not at the cutting table, not at the counting table, not on the block. Imagine that someone did, though; thought about the numbers, that is. Imagine that someone calculated and measured the cause and effect of dropping an atom bomb inside a (10) city block radius, the residual effects and collateral damage of the nuclear fallout. All the numbers are prognosticated and approximated based on studies and application of theory and analytics. That's how it is determined what resources will be disseminated to what demographic, through the census. As a matter of fact, and for the record even, The Institute for Defense Analysis, (IDA), produces research and confirmation to agencies such as the Drug Enforcement Agency (DEA), touted themselves as a nonprofit corporation That operates three federally funded research and development centers to provide an objective analysis of national security issues, particularly those requiring scientific and technical expertise and conduct related research on their national challenges. A study conducted on the price and purity of illicit drugs, from (1981 to 2007), during the years that I had been introduced to and spent in the drug trade from (1989 to 1995) confirmed that the purity of heroin in the Washington DC area peaked at slightly less than (3%) even when seizures occurred. That said, ol' boy was onto something. I'll be damned. I'll remind you that at the time when my cage partner is handing me these pearls of unadulterated wisdom, we're both trying to figure out how to obtain and push some smack as a means of freeing myself from the state of bondage. I still had yet to receive any information on the FBI's Counter-Intelligence Program (Cointelpro), The CIA Drug Conspiracy, or even the Willie Lynch "Let's make a slave" document. Knowing what I know at this point, (20) plus years later, it saddens me and sickens me that it is information, public information out there that breaks down the fact that there are a purpose and rationale behind the promotion of drug use and abuse and flooding of these illicit narcotics in the inner city, majority-black, low-income communities, but collectively, we don't know it. We hear it and don't listen. We see the drug sweeps, sometimes get caught in them, and chalk it up to the *game*. There are corporations, organizations, and institutions dedicated to studying social dis-ease that are government-funded and support law enforcement agencies with insight and quantified numbers that helped the system develop technological advancements in the war on drugs. All of this shit in place, the scientific data, the technical expertise, the federal funding for all this exquisite, logistical crap, and no end to the drug problem in this country. No one has an answer outside of locking us up; no one has found a proper response to dealing with our social ills, with all this technology and all these brilliant mutha' fuckas' that get government funding. The best that we can hope for is someone in a corporate seat fixating on how to seduce me into believing that if I sell these drugs, I can find a financial resultion to all of my personal shit; so I reach out and take hold of the very same dragnet used to entrap my own kind, that eventually I find myself caught up in. The real-time real-life perspective of a co-conspirator to fraud, robbery, murder, all committed against me.

It's insane, the depths of this rabbit hole. For the most part, the people who are considered citizens are the ones that pay taxes; taxes exist as a means to pay to be governed. Thus, citizenship funds every facet of what a nation consists of, and through these funds, ideally, the citizenship reflects or projects a national/international cultural-political identity. Apparently, it costs to be an American, but what happens to those who don't contribute to the pot, either because they can't afford to or simply don't have the means? They become recipients. Monies are allotted through institutions that identify, scrutinize, objectify, and trivialize these people and what they require to supplement their basic and most fundamental needs, i.e., food, clothing, and shelter. If you check the fine print, these people are considered second-class citizens. Second-class because they can't afford the equal protections allotted to a citizen. The tax money that came out of my mother and father's paycheck was a contribution to the welfare of the city-state and a federal bureaucracy that hand picks scholars and theorists to hypothesize the state of affairs of the lower-class and institute a means through which to maximize the economic and political value of poor people and the real estate they inhabit, all the while simultaneously perpetuating the elements that maintain a lower-class. Criminalization ensures that second-class citizenship exists so that there be an entire population of people that are almost completely subjugated to domestic labor and have little to no political control to govern their own best interests and affairs. Thus, most poor people don't vote, even if they can, because they see no true and impactful benefit. The people that they'd be voting for don't and have never represented their best image and interest. Since times immemorial, policy, law, the rules of engagement, even what's best for us, has been dictated to us. I know enough now to say that this happens because we don't invest in the process, but I also know that it is a broken process. It's a catch (22), one among the many, but to leave that level of power on the table has rendered us as subordinate to the process, making us second-class citizens by default.

The question now becomes, what happens to a person or people who don't exercise the ability to define, defend, and promote their own best image and interests? They become recipients. We don't control the flow of the information we receive, but we don't control the information. We don't infuse one another with information that will empower us enough to protect ourselves from the varying degrees of aggression we're subjected to at the hands of those who are determined to oppress and make slaves of us. Believe it or not, there was a time when narcotics weren't illegal. Once the idea of criminalizing drugs became a priority, so did the idea of criminalizing black people, then poor minorities. I've already answered the question someone asked me, saying, "Haven't they always criminalized black people?" To this, I say, "No." If they decided we were a nuisance, too black, too prideful, too *saddity, upity*, smart, dumb, fast, slow, sweaty, fat, skinny, tall, short, or visible, they'd have a lynching. The reality is that simply murdering us wasn't economically bright, but if we're made to be subjected to a supposed debt, they can kill two birds with one stone, getting rich in the process. They didn't criminalize us, though; they persecuted us and executed us. They still do, just differently, more complex to suit the times. Now we're told that we are at war. According to Robert Greene's "(33) Strategies of War," America wages war through attrition, constant harassment, abuse, or attack. This is their fighting style. Why would that change in the war on drugs? This campaign has gone on for almost (60) years. People get exhausted, their constitution weakens under the weight of harassment, abuse, and endless attacks. It soon seems like a good idea to party as a distraction to take your mind off the rigamarole. You start to party so much that its novelty begins to wane, but the alternative is to get back into the trenches. Then, on a random Friday night, someone has the bright idea to take this party to the next level, so they go for a short walk around the corner to get some party favors from the *Lil' skinny dude over there...*

Chapter 6
The Rising Cost of Freedom

Last night, I had a stirring dream that included my grandmother, one of my uncles, and a younger cousin I'd never met. Whenever I dream, and my grandmother is in it somehow, I'm always trying to have a real conversation and ask her questions that are relevant and fulfilling to me; questions about her and our family history; about me, who and what I am, and where I come from; questions about life. I never get any answers if I ever even get to ask, but I'm always trying to have this talk with her. I had just been released in the dream, finding myself in a familiar area of East Baltimore that didn't look very familiar anymore. My grandmother, my cousin, and I were on a bus going to my uncle's house, and my little cousin was acting bratty and very disrespectful the entire ride. Every time I attempted to correct this child and check her behavior, my grandmother would get on me about talking to her in that tone I use when I'm serious about what I want when I'm demanding decency. We arrive at my uncle's home, and the man is towering over me. He looks (10) feet tall, so I'm trying to hug him, but he can't lean over because he's injured his back. I explained to him that I have to leave, but I'll return later, and suddenly, as dreams go, I'm at a friend's house, in a weird-looking porch front neighborhood, where the houses are situated with a long front yard. The yards are all on a small hill, and a long trench is dug down using the hill as a barrier. Again, suddenly I'm telling my friend's mother that I have to leave, that I need to get home. The friend I'm with, whom I still have yet to recognize, explains to me that the city is at war, and one of the clicks situated in this particular neighborhood is looking for the person who killed one of their comrades. He's telling me this while he's handing me a gun and giving me directions on how to get home. I set out, and as soon as the door closes behind me, I see a dude I was locked up with, gun down another young man, then stand over the dying young man's body yelling out how he's going to find the people that murdered his man. Shooting then began from every direction, and I got into the trench intending to wait out the hostility, when the young man walked over to me and said, "Go home, O.G. This ain't your war. You've done enough. Let me have it." He stuck out his hand for the gun I was holding, gently took it from my hand, and pointed down a street that would lead me home. When I reached the end of that street, it was blocked off by a large, steep mountainside with large trees, boulders, and mud. I knew that I had to get to the other side to get home, but it just seemed impossible to climb. I looked in earnest for a way up, when out of nowhere, I saw people going into a building. I went to enter and was stopped by a man who asked me who I was. I told him, and he let me in. The building, as it turned out, was a church, and the man who let me in came up to me and said, "I know what you want, but before I let you go, I need you to set up these chairs so that the people will have somewhere to sit." I replied, "Yes, Sir.", and set up all the chairs. The man then says, "All you ever needed was the proper instructions from a man to get you to where you belong. You can go just as soon as you stack those chairs back up." I replied, "Yes, Sir. Thank you for letting me in." Then, I was jolted up from out of my sleep.

Case number (195347042). I'm in the district courthouse bullpen on North Avenue, waiting to go for a Bail Review. The similarities between poverty-stricken black folk going in a courtroom for Bail Review and black folks kidnapped and sold on an auction block are uncanny. Nothing has changed. The intent behind this auction is to set the course of the human being in line with the dehumanizing set of circumstances, slavery. Among the myriad of problems that subsist with this idea is a detail that often goes overlooked. Still, I can't quite understand why... with time comes advancements in technology, which typically is a sign of cultural advancements. Times change in the sense of it proceeding forward. However, people can get stuck in time psychologically, which affects the state of the culture socio-politically. From a cultural perspective, the dominant ideal(s) dictate the social norms, the ritualistic behaviors, the traditions, and how we address phenomena as a collective. People normally get stuck in time because of the nostalgia that connects them to certain moments, so they decide somehow to respond to change in the adverse. The point that I'm driving toward is that Europeans and European exiles in the (16th) century and beyond have enjoyed such economic success as a direct result of our *Ma'afa* (The great tragedy/The Trans-Atlantic Slave Trade) that they could do nothing less than proceed to design an infrastructure that heralds a legacy of slavery and the process of enslavement. Thus, for those who are subordinate to the colonist's rules of how this land is governed, neo-slavery and neo-colonialism are a reality. It is so deeply infused in this society that it is lawful and legitimized as a part of the systematic process through which an entire population of people became acculturated. As such, it becomes perpetual, and as a perpetual system, it goes beyond being an event. It translates as a part of the lens through which we all view our world. This world.

Here is the thing, as I'm sitting on the auction block, the thought that not (24) hours ago, I had been kidnapped, chained, shackled, and taken from my home isn't even dawning upon me. This is not a metaphor. I have just now, within the last several months, learned that I was arrested illegally and that subsequent to my arrest, my home was searched illegally. It has been (24) years now to this writing that I've been in captivity, trapped in this cage, and made to be a slave on a plantation that warehouses over (2) million people. The process of confirming me as a slave, the branding, the searing, the trial, for me, is a chilling account of what level of determination and evil is on display when people like me are born into such an eventuality. I don't say this loosely when I said eventuality; this is exactly what I mean. I'm talking about the eventuality that comes with the fact of being born black in these United States; no matter your economic station and social status, you're subject to experience racism, eventually. I didn't know how the police that arrested me used my arrest to legitimize terrorizing my entire family. Not theoretically, not philosophically, not allegorically or metaphorically, actually, factually. These detectives tore through my home with no warrants for my arrest and no warrants for search and seizure. They threatened my family upon invading the house, brandishing their weapons. They didn't knock on the door, announced themselves or their business. They just stormed in, pointing guns at my grandmother, aunts, uncles, younger cousins, little sister, and baby daughter. Months following this illegal arrest, this kidnapping, the detectives would harass my mother, showing up at her job, threatening her, in an attempt to make me confess to a crime I didn't commit. I didn't know. All of this was going on as I sat on the auction block, surrounded by all shades of black.

The ambiance is one of death, disease, rotting flesh. Newport smoke begins to fill the air from one corner of the bullpen, and it's like someone funneled in oxygen to the air passages of people who were suffocating. It was the cue for the games to begin. I've seen this all before at this point; the clicks beginning to form, the jail vets navigating the course for all the novices, the plotting and scheming in its infancy, seeing it actualized and someone being victimized. I'm a vet in my own right, at this point. I know the play, and I'm familiar with the terrain, but I'm still discombobulated from the shock of all that's happening to me right now. My world is about to unravel in ways that no one could imagine for themselves, and now, here I am. I don't imagine I'll get bail under any circumstances, but even if I did get one, the detectives stuck me up for every penny I had saved up from over the past year of my grind. I'm not even on that right now. I'm not thinking about bail, but neither are the upper (97 to 98%) of the bullpen. It has to be at least (100) of us in this one bullpen out of the four, and this isn't even the biggest bullpen in the courthouse. Nobody is down here in the basement of this courthouse, making the connection between bail review and slave auctions. No, we're in a cage, not even considering how dehumanizing this shit is. Then, the putrid fragrance of some junkie, or junkies, smoking *Cooleys* hits me, and I immediately get nauseated. *Cooleys* are cigarettes laced with crack, and let me tell you, this to me is one of the absolute worst smells I've ever encountered. Picture that; the B.O., the dragon breath, the smell of vomit, urine, feces, and cheap ass Sweaty Betty, I can live with but smoke a cracked laced cigarette, and that funk kills me. What in the fuck is going on here?! I'm at the beginning of the ending of my entire world, and I don't even fully understand why I'm here or how any of this happened to me. I was just a flat-foot drug peddler, trying to earn my way to something different, something better.

The state of Maryland versus Omar Terrell Shannon. It didn't even register. The entire state with its endless resources, versus... me? I can't afford a competent defense to argue my way out of this situation. Still, my mother and father found a way to sort out something so that I wouldn't wind up in the caseload of an overworked, underpaid, greatly underappreciated public defender, who, by the way, is employed by the same folks I'm in contention with. I didn't have enough sense to be afraid of this monster. I'm not sure what being afraid would have done back then. Still, I've grown, and in doing so, developed a healthy enough fear of the destructive nature of this beast, to respect what the depth of this really is and to drive my enthusiasm not only to fight it but to strengthen my will and my determination to win. The only option in this exchange is victory or death, and anyone who truly knows me will tell you that I plan to live forever. Such a feat is virtually impossible as a slave.

Inmate, local ID (379-671). This is what a human being can be reduced to, being itemized and compartmentalized by number, by code. This jail thing is so much deeper than an individual breaking the law and having to pay a debt to the rest of society for such indiscriminate behavior. It is about the continuance of an enterprise, the very same enterprise that just so happens to be the linchpin of our great society. But what about me? Who shall be the one to cut the check to resolve the debt by these slave owners, slaveholders, slave traders, and overseers for these many crimes that range among the worse; murder, rape, kidnapping, theft, strong-arm robbery, extortion, etc., that were and still are being committed against an entire race? Committed against me? I am being fitted for a plantation or a gravesite if they aren't the same because right now, I'm guilty until proven innocent beyond a shadow of a doubt. I'm buried in debt, buried in doubt, and if my lawyer, the prosecutor, the judge, and the jury have their way, I'll be buried in the yard of one of these penitentiaries.

I've never thought of myself as a victim because of how shameful society has made that thing out to be. Victim blaming and victim shaming is the protocol in every conversation about the slave trade. I always thought that I believe that I made a decision and that my decisions carried with them the unfortunate consequences that have become my fate. Some of both could be true, right? But being cast as a criminal, I'm being told of my propensity to be a manipulator, not that I or anyone could be lulled, shifted, or even born into degeneracy by circumstance. I wouldn't learn of the peonage system or how I'd be considered a peon until reading "The Philosophies and Opinions of Marcus Garvey" in (2001) and then being reminded of it by a friend as above the very date of this writing. If you will, indulge me for the moment and reference page (344-45) of this book; maybe you could, for a second, understand the minutia. I've never thought of myself as a peon, but by definition, this is the state in which I find myself, the state I've subsisted within for almost a quarter of a century. I've never thought of myself as a slave, but according to the law, this is what the government requires as a consequence of my defiance, disobedience, rambunctiousness, and pride. I don't know if I'd call it ironic that, in the story told under "The Peonage System" heading, in the above-referenced book, the narrators spoke of the Farmer who, "... had a lot of those peons...", and the fact that where I was sent after being found guilty and sentenced, that prison was nicknamed, "The Farm."

Inmate DOC ID (262-536/154-6763). It's no coincidence that I've spent more time in the joint than I was alive on the streets. I had the sick fortune of getting arrested by some rotten mutha' fuckas' during a year when the governor of this fine slave colony declared in a political rant, "Life means Life…" One sick individual broke the law, which resulted in everyone in his wake suffering his consequences. Yes, I said, "In his wake." The guy didn't even live to see what came back in the harvest because he committed suicide. It only takes one individual to break the law to make a law, but the nature of the oppression Is reactionary, not progressive; thus, the laws that are created aren't curatives, there meant to stop someone from doing that thing that was already done. The problem is that the act was already committed. Why would it ever be ideal to punish people based solely on conjecture, supposition, or presumption? The fatal flaw in this is that prejudice is born of such a methodology. How effective could this be, as opposed to creating a humane system that deals with people on a case-by-case basis? Of course, this is a very time-consuming effort, but I feel like because there is no panacea for correcting people from being themselves, at the very least we could take all of the time necessary to try and help one another to become better, if only for our own sake. Twenty years later, the same governor who created the unwritten policy that effectively resentenced people who were serving parole-eligible life sentences to a non-parolable sentence, testified that the policy he created was purely political and a very detrimental error on his part. His term(s) as governor made discrimination okay for the correction administrators; it also gave the Parole Commission the ability to not grant a favorable decision to an individual who is serving life, but even worse, do nothing at all, in absolute spite of what accomplishments, achievements or growth an individual has demonstrated throughout his bid. Now here I am. I'm sitting inside of a dismal situation trying to do everything I can to change the narrative of what I've been painted as in some file that is highly misleading and in many ways absolutely false, while everyone that I know with a life bid is being told the same thing by the parole board, "Come back and see us in (10) years,"..."(2) years." ..." (5) years," ..." Some of these men have already spent over (30) years in the joint. Where does that leave someone like me?

Because of my sentence, I haven't been eligible for any programs that are meaningful to the parole board or able to participate in certain vocational shops in my actual field. I'm a Barber by trade, I've just never been licensed or certified as a professional, but I've been cutting hair now for (33) years of my life. I can't get into the vocational Barber school because I'm not within (18) months of my release date. Since this has always been the case, speaking of me being a Lifer which excludes me from a lot, upon me beginning to understand myself and comprehend the gravity of my situation, I began the process of learning how to fortify myself, appease my intellect, and my social needs by developing my own programs. I found great satisfaction in digging in and realizing that my psychological and socio-cultural requirements as a man in training, across the board, mirrored those of my social counterparts, contemporaries, elder statesman, and youth. This became my work, and I performed and fulfilled the task of building everywhere I found myself; on the tier, in the dining hall, in the courtyard, the gym, on the Bluebird to court, in transit from one plantation to another, and amongst anybody who just wanted to kick their bid through an engaging conversation. The soft-spoken, introverted kid began to find his voice. I opened up and talked to people, and at once, I started to feel myself getting strong. People could relate to me, and I became a conduit for those who shared similar attributes. It was during my formidable years of manhood training when my voice became the loudest, that I became a more confident me, more audacious, more outspoken. I started to gain a deeper comprehension of decency and demanded that I be granted such, as any dignified human should on the occasion that they find themselves at the mercy of someone or some-thing that doesn't show the fortitude of empathy, compassion, sincerity, respect, integrity and ultimately love.

I've had a few points in my young life where I've had to make some dynamic and profound changes, just like every living thing under the thumb of creation. For me, most of these times were like I was being operated on, with no anesthesia, while parts of me were surgically removed; my father, my naivete, my refuge, my creativity, my family, my freedom. The God in me is making me apt to suffer long periods of pain and turmoil. I've become dogged in my pursuits as a result. But there is only one thing in this life that I want because everything that my world consists of is directly connected to that; I want my freedom. Not the freedom I once had, I want the freedom I've discovered and defined for myself. That pursuit has already rewarded me just in gaining the sheer desire to speak up and be heard. I cried out in pain when I was most vulnerable; you know that period in life when molting begins. I was unarmed, naked, and yet, still relentless. I just had to suffer the pain and deal with the rawness of my evolution. That was when I met the best part of me, that in which who has and continues to make me better. If I could do that, manifest that pure hunger, obtain, secure, maintain and perpetuate that love, all whilst in the fight of my life, all whilst in such tremendous pain, I can get freedom. I can go home. I can heal. I can help. I can... But, in the meantime, it had taken me (20) years to get over myself and read through my trial transcripts without losing it and finding those same emotions I had stifled from back when I actually had to sit through this farce that was the circus they called my trial... Case (#195347042), State of Maryland versus ... Me. As I read, I can see now what has happened to me, to us.

I don't want any misunderstandings here. Over the years, I've read my transcripts. Many of my good friends throughout the years had made the point that I need to get into my case and study my transcripts, but without guidance, context, or a clear mind, I couldn't just do that. I can't give an excuse for my lack of diligence. I can only say that, in all honesty, I used to get so overwhelmed by everything this case consisted of, the situation with its cast of characters, the fact of being found guilty in what amounted to a little more than a kangaroo court, receiving a life sentence as a result of all of this, the legal jargon and the games that were played on me, right in my face, all due to my ignorance. It was scary and very intimidating for me, reading all of this, my life, and how I was demonized due to my lifestyle, in front of my mother and my baby girl. Telling me to study this? How am I supposed to know what it is I'm supposed to see? How am I supposed to decipher any of this to find something I can exploit that would help me get home? In a way, telling me to study my case back then was tantamount to telling me to drill a hole in my head. It didn't matter how much I believe I wanted to go home; this case was an open, festering wound; my open, festering wound.

I think about this a lot; I mean, how long it's taken me to reach this level of resolve and determination. Yeah, me, the consummate picture of the rebel. Me, with my resilience. Me, with this aptitude towards all things revolutionary. I've had no choice but to question my sense of self-love. It's taken me (20) years to go all the way back to the beginning. My ignorance, the thing that became my go-to when I needed to place blame, my unlikely ally that I've had so much love and hate for, I finally had to let it go. In doing so, I had to take back all of the layers of myself that I used to protect my ignorance from being exposed, and it was in that moment that I saw that foul, nasty mutha' fucka' naked for the very first time in my life. Now, I see it everywhere. I can't unsee this shit. It shows me that my assertions about this entire system's diabolical nature are more valid than they are the borderline paranoid rantings of an angry, slighted, convicted sociopath.

Ignorance gives the system its platform. The system, more specifically, the culture, governance, education, economics, social and spiritual dynamics that we, the people, live within, is sustained through the constant and consistent promotion of ignorance. Bearing this in mind, ignorance neutralizes one's sense of autonomy, as well as a personal sense of duty and obligation to the community. Under such observances, one tends to concede and relinquish power and authority to that thing that poses the greatest threat to our personal and interpersonal self-worth. In that vein, we, the people, can only rise as high as our most ignorant from amongst us. A nigger, a nigga can level up in this society with no boundaries, no ceiling, simply because niggas pose very little to no threat to this establishment, as long as we continue to embellish this inconsistent, incongruent and insoluble behavior. What does this mean, though? In my way of seeing things, first of all, the term nigga/ nigger is not descriptive of the black mind; let's just put that out there. The system has always found a way to set us against one another to keep us vulnerable, whether through skin tone or other clever means. In this sense, though, think about how a slave owner makes a slave complicit in his own enslavement. He promotes the slave from the field, to the stable, to the house, to overseer/trustee. Yes, niggers had guns, whips. Niggers can run, but they don't. They could free the rest of us, but they won't. Niggers could infiltrate and brutalize the system of oppression to the brink of obliteration, but they refuse to give up what their master has given them in concessions, which in total amounts to absolutely less than nothing. A nigga, a nigger, is worse off than the slaves in the field because this lost soul genuinely has no sense of identity, direction, or dignity, and this is what we want to take ownership of as a term of endearment? "Nigga, please!" So, you may ask, "Why didn't you run, wit' your rebellious-assed self?" My answer is that not a day goes by when that thought isn't present. But no matter how long I stare, I can't see beyond the chain-linked fences, razor, and barbed wires. I'm afraid. I'm not afraid to go; I'm afraid of what happens next. I'm afraid for those I'd have to leave behind. If I go, who is going to set my people free? I can't run. I don't know if I've done enough to fortify those who would be left in the wake of such an event, so instead of running, the process of my liberation has to be as a result of a proliferation of ideals that are themselves systematic, but revolutionary in nature. My liberation has to be a resurrection of black unity, black power, and black love.

I don't want this to go over anyone's head. What I'm dealing with is a myriad of different things that all are rooted in role identification, social and personal responsibility and obligation, and accountability, personal, interpersonal, and systemized. This entire establishment has always been an extraordinary narrative that can only be fully explained through the numbers. Yes, my old *dope fiend* cage partner was right ... "It's a numbers game...", so let's do the math because it has come to a point now where we need to see for ourselves why this archaic prison system with its archaic ideology and methodology, is still in place. Even before that, though, let us first understand that all of this, from its very inception, is in fact, and, in deed, not only an extension of the Trans-Atlantic Slave Trade but is in fact, in deed, and memorialized in the United States constitution, which is the law that governs all people within the borders of North America under the (13th) Amendment, slavery. "Neither slavery nor involuntary servitude, except as a punishment for a crime whereof the party shall have been duly convicted, shall exist within the United States, or any place subject to their jurisdiction." ~Passed by Congress January (31), 1865; ratified December (6), 1865. In (26) amendments, the word except only appears twice. This is no anomaly; this legitimizes a concerted effort to maintain the status quo ante. The question now becomes this, when the time comes to ante up, what is going into and coming out of the pot? We, prisoners, are told that we owe a debt to society for our indiscretions, so to speak. This implies that my entire existence, especially as a ward of this system, has an exact dollar amount; which means that for every day that I spend as a legally identified slave to the state of Maryland, my presence within these walls is directly attached to a specific cost, according to what I've been convicted for and the sentence I'm forced to serve. With that, I have been relegated to three separate identification numbers that serve the same purpose as a bar code. Such as the custom when something, some product becomes part of an inventory. Since the Era of Mass Incarceration was effectively ushered in through the War on Drugs, the common practice has been to warehouse people within the Prison Industrial Complex. Thus, the human inventory must be identified accordingly. People stop being considered human, which forgives any holding that a prisoner's treatment should be humane. Furthermore, upon a person being charged with a crime, duly convicted and sentenced, they are itemized by numerical code, then classified and shipped off to the plantation they are housed. This is the law and how it is executed. In the state of Maryland, the item count of the entire state's inventory, called the custody count, is conducted at (3:00) PM every day with no exceptions. That count coming in from every state facility must match a master total count kept by headquarters of the Department of Public Safety and Correctional Services. There can be no miscount, and there will never be a discount. In the event of a miscount, the entire system is immediately shut down, and there will be no movement until that count comes in corrected. No employees can leave until that number is reconciled... The numbers... The numbers ... The numbers.

As of fiscal year (2018), according to the report published by the Prison Policy Initiative, Maryland, as a whole, incarcerates (36,130) of its residents. Among this population, every person held involuntarily is accounted for, including state and federal prisons, local jails, juvenile detention, psychiatric commitment facilities, and immigration detention. This detailed report shows that Maryland has an incarceration rate of (585) per (100,000) people. Here's the thing, the entire United States incarcerates (698) per (100,000), a difference of only (113). If I'm just looking at the map of the United States, Maryland is one of the smallest states, which makes the number of people that Maryland incarcerates astronomical in and of itself; however, and looking further into this study, this tiny state incarcerates its residents at a rate that is (4) times greater than the United Kingdom and Portugal; (5) times greater than Luxembourg and Canada; (6) times greater than France, Italy, and Belgium; (8) times greater than Norway; (10) times greater than the Netherlands and Denmark, and (15) times greater than Iceland. This is beyond ridiculous from my small point of view. Still, it stays true to the narrative that Maryland is not only a prison state but is one of the oldest slaveholding colonies, a tradition that obviously won't be broken. Here's another fact that is true by the numbers... Once you become one of the incarcerated, it becomes almost impossible to escape the stigma that comes with it. Most people in this situation were already living void of access to the necessary resources needed to cultivate a lifestyle where enslavement isn't typical of their reality. Doing a bid usually doesn't ease that burden. Maryland has a total of (117,030) convicted persons that are right now either behind bars or on parole and probation. One more rabbit hole, I know, but dig this, ... There are (71,000) people on probation, with (9,900) on parole. Now, here's the situation, in Maryland, you have a point system that determines one's security level that is broken down into categories, the length of sentence, how many times you've been incarcerated, your adjustment history, (how many behavioral infractions and the latest infraction received), and if you have a detainer, (open charges or unresolved court proceedings). This all determines your classification and what security level prison you may be housed within; ultra-max, maximum, medium (1 & 2), minimum, pre-release, and work release. Maryland has a dual parole system, which means that there are two ways to be paroled; the Parole Board may grant an individual parole, which is called or considered discretionary release, which occurs through a hearing. The second is called mandatory supervision. One obtains an early release on mandatory supervision by accumulating good conduct credits, industrial credits, special project credits, and before (2009), double-celling or housing credits. These credits are days that one earns for working various jobs in the prison they're housed within. The only exception to this was the double-celling credits, which came into the equation at the inception of mass incarceration, considering the prisons in Maryland were only designed to house (1/3) of the population it now holds. The jails became overcrowded as the War on Drugs took root in Maryland. The prison bureaucrats were grabbing at straws for solutions to the overcrowding when cages that were only designed to hold one captive was doubled up and now held two. The idea was that if one fits a certain criterion, e.g., a non-violent offender, they could earn the extra credits as compensation for being housed, on the fringes of legality, with another offender violent or non-violent. In any event, double celling became normalized, so with a dramatic push from Crime Victim's Advocacy Groups, double-celling credits were basically outlawed. Anyway, earning credits subtract from one's projected maximum release date, which creates a new date. The new date allows the individual to serve the remainder of their entire sentence on the streets under the Secretary of the Department of Public Safety and Correctional Services' mandatory supervision. In effect, you're still a ward of the state, but you're not being held under the same custody count as someone housed in a prison cell. The objective was to mimic somewhat the idea of how other states release prisoners early for good behavior. The difference is that good behavior in Maryland means you were paid these days as a part of your compensation for the job you are employed under. Also, it was supposed to free up bed space for the new slaves coming into the system. Someone is saying, "What's wrong with that? Shouldn't you have to earn these days that'll get you out of prison sooner?" Sure, you are correct, but one who doesn't know better would readily be under the false assumption that the warden gave you these days as a reward for you not being an asshole while you were locked up, which is the furthest thing from the truth. Everything you receive has a price tag attached to it. Everything is a give and take. Case in point, once a prisoner transitions through the system and they finally obtain pre-release and work-release status, he or she is charged money for room and board in that respective facility. Hell, an individual out on discretionary parole is charged a fee on parole, a fee for urinalysis, and God knows what else. Can't you see? This is indentured servitude, Man.

Why, why is any of this important? Because some genius came up with the method of perpetuating an idea on such a grand scale, that the reality, the frightening reality, is that the entire slave population never dwindles, it's self-sufficient, it maintains itself. The entire prison population in the United States, since I can remember, has always floated around (2.2 to 2.3) million. If in Maryland, the entire prison population is just under (6%) and just over (5%) of this nation's whole prison population, number one, no one touched by this system is ever freed of its grasp. For every ex-convict that doesn't become a recidivist once they are off parole, probation, or a stint, at least one new slave is being committed or convicted to servitude, who's basically taking their place. Think about that. Think about the effectiveness of a system that's so great that new slaves are being added into the inventory every single day, even as the old slaves leave the plantation and later return. For those that return, the true tale of the tape isn't that they're all incorrigible deviants or career criminals. For the most part, they were ill-equipped to handle being reintroduced to a society that had advanced greatly while this individual was in stasis for years. Despite the available programs, if you fit the criteria to participate, the system fails miserably in reintegrating people who served as a slave to this fine state. I will never believe that such a process is even meant to positively impact an ex-convict because it doesn't serve the full purpose of making money at the end of the day, for the system that had the most life-altering effect on the person it is turning loose. Recidivism is a part of the overall design. Still, I'm not going to do that thing that the media tends to do and not be objective in my assessment of the people who do become recidivists. Some people, although they are in the exclusive minority, are career criminals, but even that has a pathology, which means that we have to be careful in how we tread into that territory lest we risk mincing and mixing sound diagnosis with misconception. Recidivism is a reality, so much so that when chattel slavery became illegitimate as a social norm towards the late (19th) century because these people were released from bondage with practically nothing, many former slaves found themselves back on a plantation as a sharecropper, working for the same cruel plantation owners they've been told they could finally be freed from. I personally know people who come back and forth to prison because they can't cope in society psychologically and don't have the inventiveness the charisma, or the sheer enthusiasm to find their way on the legal side of economics. They may lack the maturity levels needed to be self-reliant, self-determined, and just flat out responsible, so instead of educating themselves or doing a productive bid; they are satisfied with living off of the provisions giving them by the state. We call them "state babies."

Recidivism, as a tool, is so deeply woven into the fabrics of this trade that the numbers, yes, these God-forsaken numbers, details how diabolical, complex, and impervious of a system we're ushered into. The rate of recidivism is the backdrop that keeps the flow steady for those invested in slavery. On the national side, about (2/3) of the prisoners released become recidivists within (3) years of being released from prison; that's (66%). The rate of recidivism for the state of Maryland is around (40.5%). How can one state carry the lion's share of the entire national average? But look at the reports, any of the reports on recidivism, and besides the numbers, the reporter explains exactly why people who've served time in prison come back. If it's not deliberate, then those states that bank on the slave economy would do the exact opposite of what they've done since the prison population boom of the mid to late (80s) and (90s). I'm talking about the extraction of the college programs and Pell grants for prisoners seeking higher learning. Prisoners were receiving bachelor's and associate degrees, studying and receiving information, education from college professors from accredited institutions, and local schools to the region they were in prison within. Men and women were taking the initiative to build themselves up and make themselves a viable asset to the very thing that they were cut off from culturally due to their systemic disenfranchisement before them being convicted of a crime; Corporate America.

If you look at Maryland's sister state, Virginia, a state that's (4x) larger, whose government invests in and promotes the installation of an entire educational system in its prisons, the recidivism rate is less than (24%). I'm not letting Virginia off the hook for their participation in this trade. I'm simply showing the numbers, which is the tale of progressive thinking and prolific action versus stubborn, obstinate, oppressive, monomaniacal drama, the same drama that started the civil war, where the southern states were determined to continue the enterprise of chattel slavery. Such a determination came at the expense of human lives, while the North, who is the supposed lesser of the two evils, wanted to usher in an industrial revolution. History says that the North won, but with a population of prisoners that is larger than the population of the city of Houston, Texas, slightly smaller than the city of Chicago, Illinois, and the entire state of Kansas, just to name a few, I have no choice but to see the (13th) Amendment within the scope that I do, as a compromise that fuels the race to criminalize as many of your states marginalized residents as you can to maintain that sense of cultural normalcy that made North America rich in the first place. The middle ground is the thing we have now, the Prison Industrial Complex, that is the best or the worst of both, depending on where you're sitting as you read this. The (13th) amended rule to the law of this land gives the individual states the right to own slaves and the full opportunity to participate in the industrialization that's advancing the rest of the civilized world. Furthermore, the federal government supports this neo-slavery by charging the US citizenship a fee to maintain the prison industry, you know, the taxes all of you good people are unsettled about. It cost about ($45,875) a year to provide food, clothing, shelter, recreation equipment, education, and health care in Maryland. On the low end, the state prison population is just around (18,000) men and women, so do the math, and what you'll see is that at only (18,000) people in prison, it cost taxpayers ($825,575,000). Again, this is just a state prison system, not inclusive of the federal system, local jails, juvenile detention, involuntary commitment, and immigration. Citizens don't receive a tax break for what they spend on prisons. None of my family members can claim me as a dependent on their taxes, despite the financial support they may send me to supplement my well-being here. Now someone is saying, "Why would anyone send you any of their hard-earned money?" I guess that's a fair question if you don't have someone you know and love who's incarcerated. I will say this, many people in the joint don't have outside support, so any contact, any relationships that can be developed or maintained is a huge blessing. You see, nothing is given for free in here, as I've already mentioned, so how does one take care of their basic hygiene if they have no money? Simple, you get a job.

In most prisons in this state, upon entering, you are classified, and case management gives you an institutional orientation to let you know what jobs and programs you're eligible for. Then you are added to a waiting list of your choice, kitchen/dietary or sanitation. Depending on what jail you're in and what time of the year, it usually determines how long you'll stay on a waiting list, but it could sometimes take from six months to a year before you reach the top of the list for the most basic jobs. Another option that some people take is GED classes. You received a day's pay for attending school, and your placement is almost immediate, so you can receive your pay and be in a position to take care of some of your basic needs. While waiting for a job, those of us who are fortunate enough may receive a money order from one of our beloved supporters. That money goes into a prison banking system (where it collects interest for the prison(s) until you can spend it on commissary for food, hygiene, stationary, and a few miscellaneous items. Since September of (2015), the commissary in Maryland's entire state was privatized by Keefe. At one time, or should I say, before (2015), an individual could live from state pay to state pay because, number one, despite the extremely low wages we made, commissary prices were compatible with a prisoner's cost of living. Since being privatized, commissary prices under Keefe have tripled. They even have included in their contract with the state that they maintain the discretion to raise prices on their products annually, use of discretion of which they have not been shy in applying every year since (2015). Here's the thing, upon me entering the state prison system, the wages have remained the same for those jobs that the vast majority of us work. This is the second decade of the millennium, and for over (25) years, the wages for a laborer who works sanitation, dietary and an individual who goes to school is slightly above ($0.11) and less than ($0.12) per hour. At (8) hours a day and (5) days a week (even though you'll more likely work all (7) days), you make a weekly wage of ($4.75), which doesn't calculate until the pay period for the month. We're talking about an average of ($19.00) for an entire month of work. No one in this state can take care of all of their basic hygienic necessities if they buy their products from Keefe, who, by the way, has been named as the defendant in lawsuits that have been filed in (22) out of (23) states. Guess who's not on the list of plaintiffs. Everyone is in on the hustle in Maryland. It's what they used to call the monkey hustle back in the day, where everybody has a stake in the *game*, but it's all a con. The phone companies, up until somewhere between (2016) or (2017), were charging a long-distance toll on calls that were not only in the same state, some calls were to towns that were (1 ½) hours' drive away; hell, some calls were to numbers that were local to the region of the jail but were on the wrong side of the toll line. Those calls, for (30) minutes, cost somewhere between (11 and 13) dollars. Now, Keefe and the phone company are linked up. It's one long chain of advanced exploitation of our family's desire to keep us connected, keep us in good spirits and a healthy mental state, but also our need to maintain a sense of being human. Yeah, that has a price tag too. As a matter of fact, my favorite game show host from when I was a kid found his way into the *game*, selling cheap toiletries to prisons. I guess the price was right.

Every year that passes since Keefe outbid every other potential vendor for the Maryland contract, the same rumor is renewed about their contract being up and Keefe being a thing of the past. No more ($8.43) bags of (16) tide pods. No more (.34) cent Ramen noodles and individually sold tea bags. I'd have to work (3 ½) hours to be able to afford one noodle. If I only ordered commissary once a month with state pay alone and didn't purchase anything but hygiene products, if I tried to buy everything I needed for a month, either I'd owed Keefe money, or I'd be a dirty mutha' fucka' for a few weeks. Needless to say, the rumors about Keefe leaving have never been true.

I'd be remiss if I fail to mention that there are, in fact, other jobs that one could obtain behind these walls because I don't want you to think I'm one-sided in my explanation. This is, in fact, a microcosm of society, and as a society, all the basic things are here; there's just no access for us to advance technologically. What this means is that we will, in fact, be behind upon being released, as it is the technology advances in such a way that every year one spends out of touch, it's like a (3) year set back. It's impractical. Thus, without exposure through education, a convict becomes vulnerable to try to exist outside of these walls. This doesn't mean that they can't or won't figure it out for themselves or even make good use of the tech; it simply means that the individual is working with an extraordinary handicap the longer they've spent in stasis. An ex-convict needs support, understanding, and the patience of his support system to give him time to adjust, adapt, and reassert him or herself into a dangerous new world. A parolee doesn't have much time to find their way and the parole system is most intolerable to an individual who can't pay their toll, so once again, we're looking at the increased probability of this person becoming a recidivist. Think about how many people you've had relationships with over the past (5) years, over the past (10) years, over the past (20) years; if you can go back that far, how many of them are still around? How many situations have occurred where there is a serious disagreement, and you've decided to cut ties and move on? An individual going to prison, for some people, is just disagreeable enough to cut them out of the picture. Time doesn't reward the disadvantaged. Time is one more on the list of the enemies...a list that, for me, includes the state of Maryland.

It sounds so melodramatic, the me-against-the-world

thing, doesn't it? I don't think that the entire world is against me; I'm illustrating that I have found myself in a world where those who have power and influence usually wield it in a way that doesn't empower those who are absolutely powerless. What happens is that the powerless become the vessels employed so that the powerful stay in control. As a so-called dope boy in the hood, I didn't know that I could take my diploma and apply for a job in corrections; somebody knew, just not me. I lived within walking distance and hustled just a stone's throw away from the Baltimore City Detention Center, the Maryland Penitentiary, the Diagnostics Classification Center, the Baltimore Pre-Release Unit, Central Booking, and all of the other jails in that centralized area. Here's some reality for you, I've either walked past or rode my bike through that entire area damned near my whole life and didn't know truly where the hell I was or what kind of hell an entire multitude of people was going through inside of that big church looking building, or that skyscraper, or that old factory looking building. I didn't know that it was slaves in there. I also didn't know that that region, right there surrounded by the projects, Forest Street, Lafayette, and Latrobe, the low-income housing, is a multi-million, close to a billion-dollar industry. Somebody knew, just not me. The power brokers in Baltimore city maintained and jettisoned a damn near billion-dollar economic base, right next door to that place where people who deal with some of the most dismal circumstances of human drama live. Rather than invest in a process that could give these people a different idea about themselves and their worldview, they use us to build their prison infrastructure, economy, and rationale. They are literally shooting fish in a barrel.

I'm constantly asking myself how I could have been so blind to the fact. It would have cost me nothing to ask questions relevant to my role and my output and how I could contribute to the world I was reared in. I wanted to question everything except what would affect me and how the world would respond to my existence as a black man born into a humble station in life. Not for nothing, what kind of child would ask such things, and who would they go to for such counsel? Shit, I didn't know that we had a station or what that meant, but somebody did, and they found a clever and very intriguing way to manipulate that to add me into a very complex economic situation, one that wasn't self-gratifying. In the long and short of it all, it's the predator/prey relationship being exemplified on levels that reach far beyond the comprehension of people who don't know they're living with impaired vision or that their impairment of sorts come from a tactical, scientific endeavor that deliberately keeps us in check and in the view of those who had developed a taste for the blood, sweat, and tears of people who can't buy their way out. Some of us have taken on this path of blaming ourselves or one another for our collective state of affairs. We check one another with the half-told, half-truths of... "We sold each other into slavery.", or "We did this to ourselves." ... I've never supported that mess, even when I didn't know any better. I just never felt that collectively we were diabolical enough to carry the full weight of such a complicated ordeal. Just learn our history. It will show you from then to now that the dynamics of slavery, the full scope of it, the thrust of his progeny is grounded in politics, economics, and xenophobia, all of which become inextricable to the cultural constructs of people who prioritize and celebrate a material world.

What if I were to say that "I am a man?" In that declaration, I would have to support such a statement with bold, comprehensive actions that are consistent with what we all agree defines manhood. But what if I were to say, "I am not a slave?" No matter how virtuous and righteous my performance, no matter how bold, comprehensive, or consistent, my circumstances say the exact opposite. An individual can't prove that they aren't a slave through acts of professionalism, especially if they are actively enslaved. In this world, you stop being a slave when you stop being an asset to the slave machine. The moment you become a liability to your captor is the moment you become a "glitch in the matrix." Thus, you must be systematically dealt with; corrected. You are corrected or corrupted, depending on your point of view before you corrupt someone else, which goes back to the notion I submitted to you before about there being no room in this system for a conscious individual. Begging your pardon, this has been my experience. I've personally dealt with the dangers that come with being a man in prison, becoming a conscious and a conscientious man in prison, and now being a man working toward liberating myself and my brethren from this state of bondage. The scrutiny I've learned to deal with has broken the fighting spirit of many good Souljah's. I'm no better than they are. I simply have a different threshold for pain and bullshit. I've developed a different sense of resiliency, not more, not less, simply different. I figured out that once I stopped making the slavers money, but even more so, start making them lose money, eventually I'll have to be reckoned with, but only appropriately this time. However, I know that I can't take as much in capital from the system as it has taken from my family and me.

Before I go any further, I want to expound upon something I said in the last sentiments I expressed about being professional. Professionalism shows the fortitude of discipline and an aptitude towards being solution-oriented, studious, articulate, diligent, vigilant, and obedient. In my experience, such people excel at being professional but are subjugated to slave status. These people are met with some of the harshest criticisms and receive the most unabated scrutiny from everyone they have contact with. Your family loses sight of your ability to grow beyond being the individual they remember from before you began developing yourself, so they don't usually know how to respond to the transformation. If you try to engage them in the process, they say things like, "You talkin' that jailhouse shit.", or they say things like, "That's that jailhouse Muslim stuff." In other words, your newly discovered path to excellence is met with suspicion, disbelief, and apprehension. Before coming to prison, I used to receive this as a child, "You too damn smart!", and, "You always tryin' to be so fuckin' logical!", and here, when talking to an overseer, they say, "You're using too many big words. You need to dumb it down." The prison administrators don't say anything, they just put their enforcers on me, and the moment I show any signs of human fallibility, they say, "I'm disappointed in you, Shannon. You're supposed to be a leader." Thus, when I say, "an individual can't prove that they aren't a slave through acts of professionalism ..." part of that is due to there being an underlying distrust for intellect on both sides of the line. I'm too smart to be the nigga I used to portray in my youthful impulsiveness, so I'm ostracized by the people who raised me, who'd rather I kept myself in that old mindset. But then, I'm too smart to remain in general population in prison because I'm suspected of being a rabble-rouser. Gaining knowledge does two things inside here; it sets you up to become an asset to your family and community; and, it sets you up to become a liability to the oppressive system you were fostered within. This isn't about being or becoming a professional slave; I don't even know what that is. It's about becoming a responsible adult using your extraordinary capabilities to dismantle an entire system and its processes from within. When you show the capacity to excel despite, that fucks with the numbers. You become a wild card, and they have to subtract (1) from everything they usually count on; one less nigga/ nigger is one less slave, one less in the profit column; one more enemy, one more enlightener, which could mean from one to thousands less of everything they usually count on. This is implying losses of millions of dollars for the system. You see, I always thought of myself as the one who'd run from the plantation; I'd be so unsettled in my soul that I'd flee in the darkest hours of the night, running, running from the whip, running from the dogs, running from the devil. No. I want that ol' devil to invite me into the big house, see me and my calm nature, and ask me in. In my mind, the path to my freedom is inside that house that sits tall on this god-forsaken land. If I run, I'll never get free. I gotta' get in that house to access the keys to the shackles on our minds, bodies, and souls. I gotta' know and understand what that old devil is protecting in that house so that I can destroy it all, from the basement to the attic.

Talking about all this destruction, all this violence makes me think about our collective fear. I pay attention to people's body language when these ideas are batted around in the various study groups and think-tanks I've found myself inside. It's like, everyone agrees that a change must occur if we are ever to procure decency, but not many people can agree on the methodology to operate through. If I explain how extreme and empathetic we need to be just to be taken seriously, in that instant, I become the radical brotha' Sefu. Let me say this, the fact that we have been convinced that this way of life that embraces neo-slavery as a state of normalcy is what we're supposed to have as an inextricable part of our culture says to me that the only change that will be resounding and effective has to be that of the most radical, most extreme. Our collective quality of life in these United States is built around our ability to entertain. That's the apex of our contribution to America's development, in the eyes of the oppressor, which comes mostly at the expense of our own cultural maldevelopment. This doesn't mean that we are only entertainers; no, we are builders. We are exemplary thinkers aligned with our natural proclivities toward spiritual enlightenment, but we become little more than entertainers without that sense of true self-awareness. I say this because our priorities are more enriching to everything that is culturally foreign to us and our need to have a cultural identity at this point in history. It's hard for me to accept that we don't know that us being here has been disastrous for us, mainly because we struggle with not having a direct historical link that predates the (16th and 17th) centuries. Now, we're just too afraid to spearhead our liberation because we don't want to lose what we have.

In that vein, what do we have? Civil rights? By definition, civil rights are the non-political rights of a citizen, especially the rights of personal liberty guaranteed to U.S. citizens by the (13th and 14th) Amendments to the constitution and by acts of congress. First of all, if I'm out of pocket on this, tell me how anybody could have the ability or the authority to impose on another human being anything that isn't in their best interests or why is there even a need to make a law that, on paper, guarantees someone's rights of personal liberty? In the (13th) amendment, it distinctly says that this so-called right is not, I repeat, not guaranteed. Miriam-Webster says that civil rights are guaranteed to U.S. citizens. If I'm considered, at best, a second-class citizen in the U.S., then such rights don't even exist for me. How can I be considered a citizen in a place that doesn't even consider me human? It's arbitrary things like this that provoke protests. So, I can be in the United States and amalgamate into its social and cultural stratum under certain conditions, most of which demand that I compromise my integrity and moral rectitude, but to what end? The Dred Scott versus Sanford decision from (1857) hasn't been remitted. As a matter of fact, the (13th) amendment was ratified in (1865), a full eight years later. The Civil Rights Act of (1964) is over a century younger than the Dred Scott decision (considered a landmark decision, might I add), but contained in it no language to disturb the ideology of the courts or those who enforce their legislation. If, in the final analysis, I have no rights which the white man is bound to respect, how do I navigate around such a violent premise? What in the fuck am I supposed to do with that, continue to be the recipient of all this hell that threatens my very existence? Something must change, and I'm not willing to wait for someone to tell me that change takes time. I'm doing time. Hell, I'm the author of time. Time bends itself to serve me, so I demand decency now, and now I'm taking that. What are you going to do? What do you demand for yourself? What are you willing to do to get it? I'm doing time for mines because some stranger came into West Africa some (500) years ago and said to himself, "Look at these niggers; I can make a fortune off of them, and they'll never know what hit 'em until it's too late." Don't you know that once a human being began to consider another human being chattel, that alone started an erosion of the human spirit of people everywhere? Now we're all tethered to that mentality somehow, you know, the mentality that establishes the grounds upon which a person should be could be or would be considered property, ... Inventory. I've been on an inventory list for almost a quarter of a century, and the only thing I've ever been guaranteed in this life is a fight to the death. Being black is one thing, but being black, poor, and intelligent hits a trifecta of enormous proportions. Being black, poor, and intelligent makes you a target, no, it makes you the target, but I'm not willing to consider what I'd be if not this.

Please don't think that these most recent thoughts have taken us away from the sentiments that inspired this entry. We are still deep into our analysis of these numbers, but we also need to contextualize the subtleties and the nuances of the *game.* I mentioned earlier the good commonwealth of Virginia, and I expounded briefly and somewhat mildly on recidivism rates there versus that in Maryland. As I stated, Virginia is, in fact (4) times the size of Maryland. The state of Virginia has within it (39) state prisons, where Maryland has (23) that are currently in operation. If you were to put Maryland inside Virginia (4) times, that would be (92) prisons. With the same population, multiplied by (4), we're looking at (72,000) prisoners on the low end. In a state that imprisoned its residents at a rate such as Maryland, multiplying the people that are counted as convicts if Maryland were the size of Virginia would surely make that number somewhere around a half a million. Of course, this is hypothetical, but what's not hypothetical is that Maryland is number one on the list of the wealthiest states in America, according to a report published by (24/7) Wall Street, where these rankings were based on data from the U.S. Census Bureau's American Community Survey and the Bureau of Labor statistics. This isn't coincidental. Maryland's economy is solid. I don't know how much of that revenue is from the slave trade because that information isn't as readily available to me as is the stats on prison cost and expenditures. It's like someone doesn't want to explain how much I'm worth in capital as if all they want me to believe about myself is that I'm just a bill; as if all they want the public to believe about the incarcerated folk, is that us being alive and wasting away in here is costing them a serious grip. I hustled for a living, and from a hustler's perspective, if I spent a dollar to make a dollar, I'm wasting my time. If I spent a dollar, I needed to make at least two. No business, legitimate or otherwise, can survive if, at the end of the day, they're only breaking even. Prison, neo-slavery, is a thriving business, putting it modestly. In Maryland, the most lucrative prison labor that exists is the shops. Formerly known as the State Use Industries (S.U.I.), now called the Maryland Correctional Enterprises, (M.C.E.). MCI-H has three major shops that consist of the meat plant, the upholstery shop, and the metal shop. These shops employed a total of (159) prisoners in (2018); (51) in the meat plant, (58) in the upholstery, and (50) in the metal shop. MCE, for the fiscal year (2018), reported the following... The meat plant made ($9,070,896), the upholstery shop made ($6,866,934) and the metal shop made ($4,217,504). This is from one prison a total of ($20,144,504). Across the state, MCE reported a total income of ($55,000,000) in sales for the fiscal year (2018). Maryland Correctional Enterprises pays its prisoner employees a base pay of ($0.20) an hour to start and maxes out its base at ($0.82) per hour. An average workday is (10) hours, and a workweek consists of (4) days, making their monthly work average out at (16) days. How much of that (20) million-plus is profit? In one year, it cost Maryland taxpayers ($45,875) to imprison one of us; if it so happens that the individual works in the MCE shops in Hagerstown, Maryland, the state, in (2018) made an average of ($126,763.10) in that fiscal year from the labors of that individual; almost three times what was spent.

These past few years have shown a rise in the call for prison reform in these United States. I have to credit Michelle Alexander for this in a major way because her work has shed light on this system for people in this society who don't come from where I come from, who under normal circumstances would have never sought out information that brings to question the politics through which they've been able to enjoy the fruits gained from slavery. Her book, "The New Jim Crow," is a game-changer for everybody. All this being said, Maryland is fighting back, holding on for dear life the threads that are deeply woven into this culture, this body politic, this economy with that, the politicians' campaign on the idea of reducing the prison population, in the midst of the opioid epidemic and the rising murder rates in Baltimore city. I'll say this; they also campaigned on promises to lower taxes, which could be done if you lower the prison population, but Maryland insists on having its slave economy, even as the rest of the civilized world is starting to realize that this generation is mature enough to understand the ramifications of dehumanization and disenfranchisement. The call for change is growing louder by the day, and yet, Maryland is steadfast and stubborn. What I see is another mutation developing out of the demand for humanitarianism. Let us not forget the (71,000) people on probation and the (9,900) people on parole. As this trend of addiction to prescription drugs persists, that population will grow exponentially in favor of reform, as will the population of people being committed involuntarily to drug treatment, inpatient programs, and institutions. The arrest rates and recidivism rates will remain consistent because the political focal point is geared around non-violent offenders. No one wants to go near a violent offender because of how that sounds as it rolls off the tongue. The stats on recidivism don't favor non-violent offenders. An individual who was incarcerated for (15) years or more is far less likely to re-offend than an individual who has served (5) years or less. But I get it; it's a matter of semantics and jargon. One person is charged with simple possession of a controlled dangerous substance; the other is charged with possession with the intent to distribute and manufacture a C.D.S. What's the difference? Well, it could boil down to one vial. What I mean is that, back when I was arrested for the first time, if a person had (15) vials or less, no matter if they were considered nickels, dimes, or anything else, it was a misdemeanor in Baltimore city. Thus, if you had (16) or more, you were charged with a felony. The felony, possession with intent, is considered a violent offense in Maryland, which was the difference in how you were classified and housed, but even before that, sentenced. I've been in a courtroom while fighting this case, chained to a brother who the judge offered him (20) years for (20) bags of heroin, at his arraignment if he would accept a guilty plea for a possession with intent charge, even though it was abundantly clear that this brother was an addict. I can't tell you the outcome of that particular case. All I can say is that, in hindsight, any of us facing a judge who has that sort of disposition left all of us at a hopeless impasse against odds none of us were equipped or even slightly prepared to deal with.

Let me be clear, the War on Drugs has had as devastating an impact on poor people, destitute communities, and people with problems as the Trans-Atlantic Slave Trade. Oftentimes, we allow human drama to lean towards one extreme or the other. The severity is downplayed or exaggerated based on who was telling the story, what role they play, and what they stand to gain from pushing the narrative in one direction or the other. Every storyteller has an objective and an angle by which to meet a said objective(s). My objective is to paint a picture from an abstract perspective that contains a structured dialogue for that part of me that yearns for disciplined thoughts. I need you to comprehend the complexities herein, i.e., the simplicity, the oversimplifications, and the lack of true insight when consideration is given to how we treat one another. Minorities who don't meet the requirements of wealth to be considered a member of the upper class, who don't earn the prescribed income to fit into the middle class, are the primary subjects to an aggressive and violent campaign to maintain a cultural anomaly that promotes degeneracy. What happens is that people who live where resources are scarce and or depleted find or create the means and the techniques they require to survive in impoverishment. Living inside of such conditions is far from ideal and is highly pressurized when considering that every human being has basic needs that must be met, or else. Quite often, people find themselves on the fringes, moving in between the lines of survival and something less, which is psychologically exhausting for a person already suffering from the exhaustion of any available resource they could think of. For some

people, the desperation becomes psychologically insurmountable, so when facing insurmountable odds in a state of exasperation, we tend to do questionable things. Some of the things we
do draw the question of legality versus what some people may
argue is just common sense. Some of us aren't quite capable of
using common sense. Add the pressure of responding to crisis,
chaos, calamity, or just plain nonsense, and you'll see that most
people fail in the clutch. I'm saying all of this to somehow help
you to visualize the plight of the lowered class. If you've never
been in desperate need of something, pray that you never have to
suffer through that feeling, but try to imagine that you have a
very limited space in which you can move freely and that everywhere you look, someone is trying to either figure out how to
maneuver in their limited space, create more space for themselves, or take your space. I promise that there will come a time
where you become preoccupied with thoughts of how to keep
what little you have. That preoccupation may develop into anxiety. Now, add that anxiety to a survivalist mentality, but also
add to that the fact that what you need to survive is mostly beyond your immediate reach, and the things you can reach is becoming less by the minute. All of us need the same thing; how we
go about obtaining those things we need is relative to each individual's perspective and worldview. The obtainment of our
psychological, psychosocial, physiological, economic, and socio-
cultural needs, across the board, from station to station, has become theater to those who have no valid connection to that experience. Such theatrical behaviors have been or become the
premise that underpins the rationale behind how we govern and
how we are governed. Paraphrasing a sentiment from Jacob Car-
ruthers's book, "Intellectual Warfare," "Our ignorance made us
the ideal slaves, in the eyes of the Europeans." Further paraphrasing a remark by Dr. Amos Wilson, who said, "It is the responsibility of the ruling class to create a society of criminals."; I reflect on
those two thoughts in particular because, in retrospect, the ruling class has struck the kind of vein that has continued to pay out
dividends by supplanting a buffet in a locked room full of starv-

ing people, but making it illegal for them to eat. We've always been viewed as less than because of our psychological disposition towards our spiritual inclinations that make our tendency to acquire materialism secondary on the proverbial to-do list. This orientation for black people, in particular, has been beaten and bred almost completely out of us. So, now they have found a way to continue to squeeze blood out of that rock by marketing to and capitalizing off that disorientation with a catch-22. The Iran-Contra scandal exposed the Central Intelligence Agency's complicity in flooding lower class neighborhoods with illicit narcotics across North America. This is the American government, selling and supplying drugs in American cities to American people, then making it illegal to do anything with the drugs they gave us. To this day, nothing has changed except for the intensity of the hunt. People are trying to figure out how to procure their need for sustenance while in the midst of being hunted like meat, and this thing hunting us is ravenous and has acquired an exclusive taste for people who personify the struggle, who persists in the face of adversity, who tried in earnest to find a way.

It's really horrifying to me, now that I'm beginning to understand that we have to go through so much pain and suffering for us to come to a sound sense of collectivity, to have a unity of purpose. It's like the idea of progress for us is a different idea from where this began for us. In one sense of it, I get it, because growing up where I did, amongst the people I grew up with, family friends, the neighborhood, our ideal of the struggle didn't reflect the Civil Rights Era or the Black Power Movement. Sure, you could trace our sense of rebelliousness back to our elders, grandparents, and parents who stood fast and gave voice to our popular concerns, but now these same elders are gone and grandparents tired. Some of our parents succumbed under the pressures of the reality of how determined the oppressor was in maintaining their cultural normalcy, so they got lax, then they got high. The higher they got, the lower we descended socially, the further divided we became culturally, which, in essence, became our depiction of the struggle. What we saw and how we identified with a concept of our collective plight was people in the streets, zombified in a way, trying to keep up or catch up with bills, debt, and hunger pains; cravings for the many material things that we imagine gives us status and entrance into a different state of being. Being rid of the rodents, the garbage, the vandalism, the polluted air, the polluted minds, the social diseases, the venereal diseases, the niggas. Our ideal of the struggle and overcoming all of what we defined simply meant finding the means through which to escape.

I'm talking about a reality that's everything but wholesome. I grew up in a household where every dinner we sat down at was like a Sunday dinner, not because of what we ate, shit, dinner could have been soup and fried spam sandwiches, but it was so many of us to feed. For us, it was the ideal way to ensure we were alright, so I appreciated that, but for all that closeness, another tale was being told behind the scenes. It's a tale of how many of us have to remain close to the center out of fear, immaturity, or an extreme lack of preparedness and having to venture out and face a world that's mean, unforgiving, and unapologetic, this world, my world. I grew up right off Monument Street, an open-air mall that spanned for about (7) city blocks of greasy spoons, fast food carry-outs, and hood fashion. All you smelled throughout the day is fried shit and incense. All you smelled at night are old grease pits, alcoholic sweat, dead rats, and urine-soaked alleys. That was home. I had no idea that I wasn't supposed to enjoy that part of where I come from. I had no idea that such a world was so complicit to the maldevelopment of all of us who lived there, even those of us who weren't so bad off, because all of us were exposed, which made all of us vulnerable. Still, today I have a deep-seated nostalgia for East Baltimore, but it's directly tied to the people. I remember Saturday mornings when everybody in the neighborhood came outside and cleaned up. The whole neighborhood was competing for the cleanest block, so we got out there, all of us, the adults, the children, the granny's and pop-pops, the aunties and uncs', the winos, the gossipy ladies, the low budget hustlers, the old, the young, all of us. The winner got a block party thrown by the city. They'd block off the streets so no traffic could enter or exit, they'd set up huge barbecue grills and a sound system for music, and we'd party all day and through the night. Of course, it was cool for the block to be clean, but it felt good that we all got together to make that happen, even if we didn't win. Those were the days of penny candy, chasing the Mr. Softee truck, passing love letters to that weekly crush...

...We traded all of that off in a very real way for a world of catastrophe. We shook on a bad deal and are now still dealing with those consequences from over (500) years ago. I often find myself angry at myself for not being courageous enough to challenge myself and my immediate circumstances in the same matter that I did upon me coming to prison. It frustrated me to no end, listening to the prosecutor in my case described me as some criminal, some low life, some despicable creature and basically called me a nigger, then had the judge join in on the fray. I think back to my trial attorney and how he never investigated my side of this case, at the very end, served me up because I refused to plead guilty, which would essentially get him off the hook for doing a piss-poor job of humanizing me, let alone representing me. All of this, and then you add into the fact that my response, no, my reaction to my immediate circumstances could only be interpreted as the behavior of some criminal, some lowlife, some despicable nigger; but what gives them the right to call me on my shit? Part of the problem is that my ignorance and the depths of it was where I received my epiphany. Calling me a nigger, treating me like a nigger, all that did was piss me off, but at that point, I honestly had no way to defend myself. The truth is, I, in fact, embraced the attitude that "'Real Niggaz' do real things" is an adage that not only should be adopted but exalted. Here's the reality, take it or leave it, real niggaz' have real problems. Those problems began the moment that nigga/nigger becomes sublime, and now, I'm actively trying to escape that branding.

Our overall plight is so riddled with problems rooted in a

total lack of spiritual congruity and comprehension. We don't care about each other enough to demand and force change in a way that creates a profound and definite cultural shift. We request changes in policy but don't change the dynamics that the policymakers have had the luxury of operating through, so it takes decades for new ideas to resonate. By that time, if there was a pressing matter, the novelty of it has waned. People forget and settle into a behavior pattern that reflects the attitude that people take on when they feel like their individual input doesn't matter. As a result, an entire collective falls into a state of categorical digression and underdevelopment. Whole communities are underserved due to a lack of belief that policymakers are genuinely concerned about their well-being, so they don't vote, but more importantly, they don't take the initiative to raise future policymakers from their grassroots; people who not only reflect our best image but who promote our best interests. The closest we've had on a national level was the Obamas, who, in the final analysis, faced so much opposition and outright disrespect, that we all are worried constantly about when and how the legacy they left will be either white-washed, dialed back, or totally obliterated from history. Part of what Mr. Obama started was more resounding culturally because it is more and more focused on the need to be civilized by executing acts of humanitarianism. Of course, I'm talking about Prison Reform. By rescinding federal crack cocaine laws, Mr. Obama essentially reversed one of the most vicious and overtly racist practices of modern-day slavery. This change, along with a comprehensive dialogue surrounding "The New Jim Crow: Mass Incarceration in the Age of Color Blindness," is the beginning of a breach in the old values and ideas that established dehumanization as the cultural norm. Some people are beginning to see and understand that the concept of penitence has been transmuted to the execution of punishment and punishment alone. The idea of contrition and rehabilitation just doesn't compute. Up until the embracement of the opioid epidemic, rehabilitation of the criminal mind or the criminal eyes didn't have, as an attribute, the same perpetual means of generating its own economy. Things are changing, and from that, I'd be willing to bet that the same people invested in prison economics have started investing in detox and rehabilitation clinics. At this point, it's the only move that makes sense, according to the numbers.

I want to ask, "What's taken so long?" without the tone of not being grateful. I want to believe that it's "better late than never," but in my heart, "never late is better." Why, after (2) decades and beyond, has it taken so long for someone to notice how much damage is inflicted on a person who spends weeks, months, and sometimes years on segregation. I've learned that you treat a person in the way in which you want them to behave. To function in opposition to the idea of propriety, in this case, simply respecting the humanity of someone else, despite their overall circumstances, mentally, emotionally, even socio-politically, economically, etc., in my mind, says that you, as the one in position, to exercise propriety or appropriateness, has problems. To be blunt, I've been a Dog Handler, training service dogs for disabled Veterans, and I'm currently in the employment of Happy Hounds Rescue Dogs Prison Program, training rescued dogs; I have seen some of the most dreadful, miserable C.O.'s come out of pocket with exclusive dog treats, bring trays full of roast beef, roast chicken, deli meats and such, to feed the dogs. These same officers will go out of their way to take an (8) ounce carton of milk from a prisoner who simply wants to eat a bowl of cereal. You see, Keefe sells bags of bargain brand generic cereal for ($3.52), for a (20) ounce bag, and ($3.59) for a (10) ounce bag of powdered milk. At least one meal a day out of the three will have milk with the meal, so if a man wants a cold milk with his cereal, what's the problem with that? Some people treat animals better than they treat other people. Some people treat other people like animals but expect these same people to behave in a dignified way while suffering abuse at their hands. How does that work? Simple decency doesn't cost one red cent, but the moment you decide that it's okay to treat someone as if they're less than human, ...I don't think anyone can afford the toll that such behavior(s) take on them spiritually. Thus, that lack of spiritual congruity I mentioned earlier. What we're examining right now is the fact that an entire group of people have been subjugated to enemy status and drawn into an actual war, where due to their/our placement on the American social ladder and economic classification, we've been targeted for attack. Placed under that state of duress, what is an appropriate response to being violently harassed, beaten, killed for simply trying to figure some shit out? What do you do when you realize that all your anxiety, your angst, your stress, is a result of the aggression being leveled at you because you were born into the role of prey? Ask yourself if you'd be overwhelmed. We've all probably seen footage of people in other countries who've been relegated to that same status, how they turn out to protest, and how the protests level up and the military is sent in to break up the unrest. Some of those folks gather stones and throw them at those soldiers who come armed and armored in full regalia, suited, and booted for a fight. The outright angry civilians losing their civility start beaming these stones at tanks, and just before the explosion occurs, the scene is cut back to the reporters who sit safely at the station's newsroom desk, twisting your ideas, manipulating your thirst for drama. They call these poor folks Rebels and show you the aftermath of that tank's destructive calling forth; the outstretched corpses of our brethren in the streets, who dared demand decency from those who've taken an oath to care for us, to keep us safe. For those who didn't perish in the streets, we're carted off to a farm and committed to peonage. I threw my share of stones at the penitentiary. I found a way to rebel and didn't even realize it. I was born a rebel by sheer fate, conditioned in the womb to go against the current. Who knew? Momma? Pops? Nah. The Judge? Yeah...he knew...

In the final analysis, we must resolve all of this. We have so much to sift through individually that it seems as though our collective plight is light-years away if we even believe that there's such a thing. Let me say this right now; there is no panacea. I don't have all the answers; no one does, but what I do have is direction. I'm not one of those people who subscribe to the notion, "I gotta get myself together before I can help somebody else." Actually, I hate that entire idea, because it's the proffer for this other thing people say, "...I'm still not satisfied with where I am right now." To the last part, being dissatisfied with where you are right now is in itself a redundant utterance because as an ordinance of life, being alive is being in constant motion. That motion is one of progress or digression. One may say, "Well, what about stagnation?" Stagnation is also a kinetic process, but not of advancement; it is a state of deterioration. Dissatisfaction is a catalyst of change, and change is evident though not always apparent. If you're not satisfied with something, typically, you bust a move in one direction or the other. Some of those moves may be bodacious, others, more subtle. As for that initial idea, "...getting myself together, before, blah, blah, blah,...help someone else", I ask this, "On what occasion will you or any of us be able to get our self together without the full and total utilization of those essential elements that are the working constituents of the togetherness you're trying to achieve?" In other words, the self is already together, but through all this systemized, categorical drama, we lost touch with that level of comprehension. Self is personal and interpersonal. Self is an individual part and extension of the collective whole and is an inextricable part at that. To sever the connection between the personal and the collective or interpersonal self is tantamount to self-destruction. What I'm saying is that, if we don't adhere to, consider, respect, and give reverence to our connectivity, we'll find ourselves in a perpetual state of dysfunction; the kind of dysfunction that we're reveling in right now, saying that we're trying to get ourselves together, but unwilling to come together to get it done. In my mind, if you're not satisfied with where you are right now, good, but ask yourself, when will you be satisfied enough with yourself to help somebody else?

Someone out there will stumble across this document and oppose maybe all that I've expressed herein. That's cool, but I must ask that you simply ask one pertinent question of yourself and even anyone else you may share this information with... "As an individual proponent of anyone who shares in common my worldview, after being exposed to this particular dialectic, how can I successfully navigate the course towards the furtherance of my life pursuits without giving genuine consideration to the perspective of the other guy?" You see, for me, this entire narrative doesn't hinge upon one's belief or disbelief in any of my experiences, my thoughts, or ideas. This is more of personal analysis of my current state of affairs in that I have to question and challenge my confinement and all of what that consists of. In the book, "Four Arguments For the Elimination of Television," author Jerry Mander, on page (122), in the section titled, "The Colonization of Experience," under argument II, offers the following premise, "Confinement itself, the removal of a creature from its natural habitat into a rearranged world where its ordinary techniques for survival and satisfaction are no longer operative, produces several inevitable results: (1.) The creature becomes dependent for survival upon whoever controls the new environment. It will use its intelligence to learn whatever new tricks are necessary to fit that system. If it takes tricks and changes to stay alive, then that's what it takes. (2.) The creature becomes focused upon (addicted to) whatever experiences remain available in the new environment. (3.) The creature, therefore, reduces its own mental and physical expectations to fit what can be gotten. Confined creatures that cannot fit this pattern go crazy, revolt, or die." I now ask if it's safe to presume that all of us live in some sort of confinement, though it may never come to pass that you be relegated systematically to the status we've come to identify as 'slave'? Are you confined to an ideology? What about a lifestyle? What exists out there that frees you, even if only for a moment? Do you understand how and why you've been classified, and do you accept that classification as a part of your identity? If you don't accept, what have you done to change how you are identified? What about you separates you from the rest of the herd? Why should you be respected? I've come to the realization of a few things about myself, but when it came to the point where I had actually to come to grips with being considered (1.) an item, (2.) a piece of inventory, (3.) a slave, (4.) an enemy of the state, rather than try to fit into the pattern that is typical of a creature in confinement, I began the process of developing my own pattern to be confined within since by sheer fate I am going to be confined to something. Some years back, I had learned to play chess. I wasn't very exceptional, shit, to my own standards, I wasn't a very good chess player at all, but I played for a while, actually until I got sick of it with boredom. There are other personal reasons why I stopped playing, but for now, I won't go all into that. People love chess. Some people equate the game of chess to the game of life. Those people are your intellects and some sort of self-enriched, self-absorbed, and self-proclaimed scholars. I've actually grown a sense of disgust for chess. It's a game of confinement and strict limitations, boundaries, and borders. I've learned that I'm a different sort of thinker, so I started on a "thinking outside of the box" campaign until I came into contact with "Game Theory." I enjoy game theory, but I still need to push those ideas beyond the set limits. I don't want to study the game anymore, so I study the mind that developed the game. The idea of its immeasurable vastitude motivates me to push beyond being a contestant in a game designed for everyone to lose. When you play chess, you expose your mind's inner workings and motivation to your opponent and anyone spectating. The only way that I was truly able to comprehend the game was to take myself off the board. I had to get a bird's eye view for me to see what I was doing and all that I did; to be able to measure my progress according to my many, many failures; all of which were due to my lack of prudence, my lacking in attention to detail, my lack of studiousness and my stubborn silence.

I said before that I was born a rebel and basically didn't realize it. I couldn't reach that realization until I realized that I was in confinement. People say, "They can lock-up my body, but they can't lock-up my mind," but if you've tried to pay attention to any of what was written herein, you'd see that there's no use here for your mind. In fact, being intelligent or cerebral inside here is a problem. I was at a point in this journey of mines where I just couldn't figure out why I was the consummate trouble magnet, and quite often, such questions concerning why I received the shit end of everything all of the time would leave my sanity just within arms' reach. I'd be fighting with myself, wanting to let go and lose my entire mind, but it was in those moments that confinement became something more than virtual. Confinement became my strange bedfellow, my ally. I can determine my own destiny, but I can also determine what processes will facilitate the bringing forth of a man, free from all forms of confinement. I've been confined to these pages for as long as I can remember. Now begins the struggle for liberation. Now begins the revolution.

When I was (24) years old, in the Maryland Correctional Institution in Jessup, I met this older gentleman on the tier I was housed in named Robert Eggy Mayo. For some reason, this old dude and I connected and developed a friendship. He used to catch me in stride, on my way to doing something counterproductive, and he'd pull me to the side and talk my whole head off about things that I didn't know I was supposed to care about. The thing that drew me in was that the way he would talk to me, in a lecturing type of tone, reminded me of Momma, my grandmother. Eggy and I spent a lot of time talking about the known and unknown, the seen and the unseen. He was a wise old guy who taught me a lot before I left MCI-J in (2001). I took a part of him with me and still hold him in high esteem right in this very moment. Not long after I left that spot, I got word that he died. A few years later, while in W.C.I. in Cumberland, Maryland, I had the occasion to meet another wise old dude by the name of Mack. Before we ever exchanged words, I noticed this familiar glimmer in his eyes. His mannerisms, his walk, and the way he talked reminded me of Eggy. They could've been brothers for all that they shared in similarities. I stayed close to Mack, absorbing the information he had concerning the world we lived in compared to the world we left, lessons in civics and social studies that were nothing like what I was taught in school. I needed those guys from that gener-ation to make right in providing me an opportunity to go through a proper rite of passage. When Mack got sick all of a sudden, I was allowed to sit with him in the hospital until he was unable to see. Then, not many days later, the C.O. who permitted me to sit with my friend told me that he was gone. Neither Eggy nor Mack saw the world outside beyond these chain-link fences, razor wire, and guard towers, but they both saw enough in me to invest the last years of their lives in my process. I miss them old dudes, to say less, but I'm almost certain that so much of the spirit they had, with their willingness to take on a young protege', and in their own way defy this state of confinement, is a part of my rebellious disposition now. If they've left me with nothing else, they've left me determined not to let this become the last view I have of the world. For that single gift, I can never be thankful enough. Now, thinking back to that dream I had, they both might've been the same man, you know, that man that let me into the church, mak-ing me responsible by testing my dexterity, my sincerity, and composition. This is the path to my freedom...Thank you for let-ting me in...

April 20, 2020

Afterword

May 31, 2020

In the time since completing Volume III., we have been struck by a global pandemic, a new form of coronavirus, being called COVID-19. As a result, life as we know it has been critically altered. Socio-cultural, socio-political, economic, educational, etc. Institutions have been shut down almost completely. The leaders of this superpower don't have solutions, and from the top down, people are in a state of loss not experienced by this generation before. People can't work, so they can't pay their bills. The government has placed moratoriums on rent, mortgages, cell phone bills, and other essential bills, but soon, that grace period will be over. *Dirtbag* landlords are already lining up with hundreds, if not thousands, of names of people to be evicted. People are falling ill with this disease, but not just physically. The saturation and at times over saturation of COVID-19 in and by the media outlets have truly driven us to the brink. This is a weird time. Panic and hysteria are the new norms due to constant speculation and rampant misinformation. No one, not doctors, not scientists, or even pathologists, has a clue as to what this novel coronavirus is, how to stop it, and as time wears on, we're learning that they aren't even certain as to where it came from.

In a very real way, being in here isolates us as prisoners from this plague, physically. Psychologically, however, this situation has heightened our sense of hypochondria and the level of worry we have for our loved ones. The only way we could contract this disease is if a state employee, contractor, or volunteer brings it into the institutions, or if a prisoner leaves the institution for court or a medical emergency to the hospital, gets infected, and comes back to the prison. For all intents, if COVID-19 protocols are followed, we are *safe*. The problem is this, this disease is something no one has ever had to deal with, so these *protocols* are constantly changing; constantly as in daily, which essentially destabilizes the very fabrics and foundation upon which a person living in a state of confinement learns to and must rely upon to survive, ... routine.

Some of us have adopted the ideal of civility to embrace the requirement of all human beings, all life, to live in a way that maintains the social contract. From this point of view, civil in this sense means law, and where there is no law, there can be no order. From sunrise until night's end, our day is organized around a set schedule, wherein every event, work, education, diet, and recreation is all fit into a set order. For many of us, any disruption of that order is tantamount to serving up chaos on a platter. This is because if ever one decides to *buck* the order, for whatever reason, consequences are soon to follow. No one wants to deal with consequences when we're thinking clearly and if we're being honest. Now our lives have been thrown into complete disarray as the people outside (Uptown) are now being made to find ways to survive the onslaught of ignorance, unemployment, media endorsed psychosis, and anxiety. Suddenly, DC jail gets blitz with an infestation of COVID-19 cases, then JCI and MCTC, and the Maryland Prison System go into quarantine. Routine, any semblance of order and all commonsense approaches and reasoned, calm, logical, and organized thinking is left to the prisoners to pursue and uphold. Imagine that. They have effectively given the maniacs the run of the asylum, in a way. Courts are closed, there are no transfers from jail to jail, no cell moves from tier to tier, and we get fed in our cages all three meals every day. It's become virtual segregation, wherein all out of cell activities have been dialed back to maybe an hour a day. We are driving each other crazy from overexposure to one another's hang-ups and bull, so we have to be ever so mindful and extra careful not to create the type of drama for oneself that could ruin years of hard work, diligence, and discipline. It is in that vein That we find ourselves in a very unique and yet very precarious situation. Our overseers are overworked and exhausted, so unlike no other time in my (24) years (6) months and (29) days, they are relying on the 'men' Confined within to set the tone for a state of collective consciousness and order amongst ourselves. The stress levels in here right now are ridiculously high, and all we can do is sit in here and gain weight, watch the news for more bad propaganda and wait for someone to bring us back some form of what we consider normalcy. For now, nothing is moving, so we are hypersensitive to every announcement that comes over the P.A. system and the horrible rumor mill that remains (99.9%) inaccurate; we call it "Inmate.com."

In all of these years, I've never been in an environment where the morale was this low but it's not just the prisoners' morale; the staff is at their wits end, and I can honestly say that all of us are in desperate need of a win. It's been since March that we've been shut down, so to speak, all day, every day, and every waking moment is filled with questions, rumors, and more speculation. I've been thrust into the position of housing unit Rep, as well as acting *Tier Rep*, so all day long, I'm fielding questions that all began this way, "Brotha' Sefu, have you heard, ...? or, "Brotha' Sefu, did they tell you, ...?" I've never been tasked with having to put out so many fires in my life. So much is happening, but my attention has been drawn to our employment status across the board. Again, everything has been dialed back, so if you're not *essential* to prison operations, i.e., sanitation, some dietary workers such as cooks and line workers, groundskeeping and recycling, or maintenance, your work status is on hold. MCE workers are out of work because, like many other job details here, they have contract employees who can't enter the institution. What this means is that the prisons are now not only unable to generate money, but because we're under this COVID protocol, the prisons expenditures on food, maintenance, and sanitation supplies and chemicals have dramatically increased, so with nothing coming in, the state prison system, as a whole, is hemorrhaging money. The industry is shut down, and it is now, if one is totally objective in their view of the prison system, that one cannot turn a blind eye to this being a system of warehousing humans.

It's funny to me that I've always accepted the premise that we, prisoners, are being warehoused by the state and can easily articulate why and how, in my mind, this premise becomes an empirical truth. The funny thing about that is that I've never gone into a full breakdown of the word *warehouse*, which is rare for me, but many of us can't, or we struggle with making the correlation between us as prisoners and the definition of warehousing in support of the notion. We've taken to the simplification of the idea that it means, "They're just holding us in here for years and years, without rehabilitating us." Warehouse is a compound word, ware, and house. Miriam-Webster, in the third text, under ware~ (1.) b: An article of merchandise; ... (3.): An intangible item (as a service or ability) that is a marketable commodity. In the second text under 'house'~ (1.) a: to provide with living quarters or shelter; (2.): To encase, enclose, or shelter as if by putting in a house; (3.): To serve as a shelter or container; contain... The first text of the word, 'warehouse'; a structure or room for the storage of merchandise or commodities; ... second text, under (2.): To confine or house (a person) in conditions suggestive of a warehouse. This all adds weight to the idea of imprisoned people being considered items, actively being itemized, and being considered merchandise. It's never been more apparent. However, the longer we are made to sit idle, the more it costs the state. Needless to say, after several weeks of placing more stringent COVID protocols daily, due to the increasing COVID cases on the streets, they still found a way to send about half of the MCE guys back to work. It was just a matter of time, but time is money, right?

I wrote this book because it was necessary, and it was time. This year of writing was one of constant reiteration, confirmation, and validation as I became more informed about my personal situation and our overall circumstances. As I'm writing this, people are in the streets. They're protesting the murder of a black man named George Floyd at the hands of (4) members of the Minneapolis Police Department. Once again, someone took the initiative to film another incident of police brutality, but this time, unlike any other time before, the world was called forth to witness a man, a black man, have his life literally squeezed out of him as the officer preceded to kneel on this man's neck. Officers of the law, yet again, have bored out, through their actions, the bottom line of American justice, the essence of American values, and the undeniable truth of American principles and priorities... How soon we forget the multitude of lives taken at the hands of people who have taken an oath to be enforcers of a malevolent, acrimonious plutocracy that maintains an ideal that divides its citizenship according to race, gender, religion, economic station, political persuasion, etc., to promote a fallacy. I think back to (1992). I was (16) years old when Los Angeles erupted. Police brutality was the catalyst, but racism was the crux. Twenty-three years later, Baltimore City, my city, among others, where our children took to the streets to demand decency, explaining to the world that "Black Lives Matter" because of the many instances of police brutality that has been the cause of death for far too many. Racism was the crux. As I watched the rainbow of races pour out into the streets in (2020), my heart pounds as my chest tightens as I hear George Floyd, while his body is desperately struggling to take in air, he manages to say to his captors, "I'm going to die.", and in the next few moments, cry out to his already deceased mother ...

Freddie Gray cried out. Eric Garner cried out. Philando Castile, Breonna Taylor cried out ... I start my mornings now listening to Kendrick Lamar's song, "Mortal Man" from his album, "To pimp a butterfly." I lay still, flat on the concrete floor, absorbing the lyrics and letting the music soak up into my skin. I let myself drift away into the rhythm, mesmerized by this stranger's ability to tell the world my life's story over a (12)-minute track of lyricism, poetry, and dialogue. I allow my mind to blacken and open up into a sort of nothingness that's akin to the furthest reaches of outer and inner space until I can no longer feel the floor beneath me. The blackness, ... The substance through which all creation was brought forth; I become one with it once more, and I cry out. I cry out until my voice breaks off from exhaustion of all the air from my lungs. I inhale deeply, replenishing these same lungs with more of the rancid, polluted oxygen that carries through it the ghosts of all the men, women, and children who've perished at the hands of evil. I cry out loud, as loud as I can in the confines of this cage, I cry out, and then I pray, my tears pouring out of me, libation that I offer the ancestors in the venerable names of my brothers and sisters ...

Our brutalization is historical; it is tremendous, and since the murder of Mr. Floyd, I'm hearing white America talk about "being *woke*" now. I'm hearing them say, "I didn't know" ... I'm hearing them apologize for their *privilege*. I don't, nor would I ever presume to know what another person knows or doesn't know. Still, I would never be convinced that any adult living or dead doesn't have any formal or informal knowledge of the black experience in America. They may not be equipped with the fortitude to empathize with the black experience, but they know. Hell, they've co-opted the black experience piecemeal for years. Now the world is hearing our cries. This is America. A dynamic place with diabolical history. People say, "Stop dwelling on the past." That didn't apply to the prosecutor when he used my prior conviction for possession of cocaine to convince a jury to convict me of a murder I didn't commit. History doesn't come to my aid to explain away our social ills and connected to our being brutalized, terrorized, raped, robbed, abducted, and murdered; no, I shouldn't dwell. Tell that to the business owners and managers who I'll apply for work from. I shouldn't dwell on the past... Maybe I shouldn't, but neither should all of those Confederate sympathizers; I mean, to say that I am suffering from my own personal instance of police brutality that even after (25) years, won't allow me to sleep through the hours of (6-7 AM); sure, let's not dwell, let's just chalk it up, I mean, hell, why should I be asleep at that time of the day anyway? What would happen if you were asleep, someone sneaks into your home and wakes you up yelling, pointing flashlights and guns in your face? Then they abduct you, while you're under the impression that all of this is above board, just a formality, you know, part of the game; what would you do when you realize that you are in fact a victim, but the realization is a quarter of a century-old? I think you'd dwell. I think you'd cry out.

"From Revelations" is my awakening, our awakening. I write to give voice to the pain. I write to find resolve. I write for love. We live in a world that creates dichotomy and then uses it to justify oppression, suppression, repression, and ultimately bloodshed. There is a sickness in us that allows ourselves and our brethren to function outside of righteousness without consequence. At every juncture in history, ancient or recent, by the time people decided to protest, it was because they'd had enough. We can't afford to keep waiting until we've gotten fed up before addressing abuse and brutalization. By that time, more lives are lost. People have to be determined not to allow public servants to enforce racism. Ask yourself, "How much has to happen in our world before the next incident being protested is surrounding you, your children, your spouse, siblings, or other family members?" When it happens to be a member of the human family, it's happened to your extended family, and that's more than enough. It's unfortunate that George Floyd had to die to shock the rest of the world into a small view of our reality. It is unfortunate that Rashard Brooks had to be murdered for us and everyone else to get fed up and demand decency. Still, I thank the Creator, in the spirit of our ancestors who lived, died, bled, shed blood, and sacrificed, for allowing the world this opportunity to redeem itself through George Floyd...

...Nothing has ever been taken from someone with the intention being to, at some point, give it back. Lives have been taken. You can't get that back, not from the deceased; therefore, take from our brutalizers their power and influence, and don't stop. If you're in the streets right now, don't stop ... Don't stop until the system of racism is dismantled completely. It's been said that these are uncertain times. I disagree ... In fact, I don't think that any other time in our shared history has had as much certainty as right now. Thank you, George... It is now in your venerated name that I cry out... Hotep!

Acknowledgements

In the venerable spirit of our ancestors, who laid the illustrious foundation upon which we now stand; who lived and died, bled and shed blood, sweat and tears in honor of the future generations; who tread vigorously the path that is our struggle for life, liberation and the exemplification of truth, balance, order, justice, harmony, propriety and reciprocity in all of our affairs, personal and interpersonal; who will forever be the criterion of righteous resistance to oppression; who instilled within us the dexterity to stay the course in the face of adversity and tumult in spite of the admonishments of our enemy. Our ancestors, who breathe into us the determination to define reality for ourselves by redefining our perceived reality and represent that definition against circumstances and conditions that are non-conducive to revolution ... It is in this spirit that I make the following acknowledgements, ...with all that is currently happening in our world's and to our worlds, I find it difficult to list the many individuals who have impacted me, my outlook, my mentality and spirit in all of the profound ways in which all of you surely have, at every juncture that my life consists of. I am bound by duty to be the very best representative of the gifts you've bestowed upon me, thus the production of this book to its completion. I'm finding my thoughts are being intruded upon by the current state of affairs, (what they call "news"). None of the events of today are "new" to the black collective. In fact, this "news" is a commentary of the history of America in brief. It is due to this history, that black people throughout the diaspora are they only people who constantly need validation and confirmation about who and what we are and what we've done as contributing members of the human family. Every other people can focus on advancing their culture(s), while we have to be convinced that we are descendants of Africa and furthermore, that Africa, (Alkebu-lan), is a great place from which to be rooted. We have to constantly be mindful enough to empower the idea and ideal that black is indeed beautiful but not only that, we now need to also be able to explain why. Every time one of our children utter the acceptance of the term nigga, it speaks to the need of that validation of our wisdom, strength and beauty; the need for a reiteration of qualitative values and lessons in our struggle to be respected as human beings. Don't simply exclaim "Black Lives Matter", explain to those who don't know why black lives matter and then live in a way that doesn't blur those lines ever again, so that no one can ever again make the tragic mistake of believing otherwise and then acting on that belief. The time for token victories is over. Our enemies have known since times immemorial that they were working on borrowed time, and though I respect how they made use of that time, they're realizing that time is up and a new era is being ushered in, with the help of their children towing the line...

... To my leaders, teachers and guides that have spanned my lifetime, our work is just beginning. To my Fatiu family, my Komrades, please know that my travels throughout this systems have been vast, but the work consistent faithful and with an undying revolutionary enthusiasm. Counterclockwise...

...To my biological family, descendants of Simms, Shannon, Wright and all-extended kin, one day, it'll all makes sense, and on that day, you'll understand who I am and what I came to do.

... To my Walker and Crudup family, your love and embracement has been unparalleled. We are indeed one.

... To the men I've souljah'd with in "the trenches", it has been my honor to walk, talk and break bread with you. I have been blessed to have received lessons at your feet. I must ask that you forgive me for not calling each and every one of you by name. I tried and the list was just so long that it became an impossible task to complete. I simply don't want to be remiss, however, all of you know where we've been together in this struggle, MCI-H,

('96-'98), (2012-'18), MCI-J, ('98-'01), (2010-'12), MCTC, ('01-'03), WCI, ('03-'06), (Aug.'12-Oct.'12), MHC, (2006), ECI, ('06-'10), RCI, (2018~), you know what we've done and what we've been through, the highs, the lows, the laughter, the tears. If we connected you know it was genuine; If we built on random ideas attended study groups and think tanks; if we were neighbors on a tier or cage partners; if at any point our friendship was more of brotherhood, know that I have not forgotten you and will never. Thank you for allowing me to serve. "I am because we are and because we are, therefore, I am."

... To my daughter, struggle is an ordinance that nothing in life can sidestep. Your childhood has prepared you well for the difficulties that come with being a Queen. Use those lessons and wear that crown high and dignified. Our time is coming, and history will be yours to make. You are a remarkable, talented, independent young woman,... my twin.

... To the four exceptional, gifted young men in whom I am honored to call sons, I hope that despite the circumstances I have been able to inspire you just as you have inspired me, my walk, my work and my vision...

... Soul sister Dominique and Eddie, Bashi Rose and family, Queen Mother Navasha and Fanon, your friendship, loyalty and sacrifices on my behalf will never be forgotten. I am forever grateful...

... To my Betterer, you continue to be more than I deserve. "You are the atoms in the air I breathe." To say more would only limit the truth of what you are... my everything... my love. Through you I see forever.

Tumalize Duara.

In honor of those beautiful spirts from the past, those who stand and fight today, and the righteous leaders and soldiers to come...

...To the four beautiful spirits who chose me as their mother. My greatest honor...my greatest creation... Qujuan, Pharez, Kenan, Jonas...you are the stars in my universe.

...To the young Queen, this fight has always been with you in mind. It's been a long, vicious, battle but victory is on the horizon. Stay inspired.

... To the next generation, Aydah, Makena, Yalriana, Alreise, we pray that the work we do now will make this world a better place for you in the future. You are the legacy.

...To my beloved Sista-Cuzn, Tammy, my family, earthly and spiritually, extended family and friends, I appreciate your love, laughter, wisdom, prayers, guidance and protection. Thank you for having a part in my life.

...To Mathew, my partner and fellow comrade. I am marveled and humbled by your magnificence daily. You are wise beyond your years. I'm so grateful for our friendship. Our connection is kismet. Our work is 4Truth.

...To my Betterer, you've inspired me in ways I've never imagined. In you, I see black greatness. In us, I see black excellence. My Lion...my everything...my love. Through you I see forever.

Pelu ife

References

Department of Public Safety and Correctional Services (2018) *Maryland Correctional Enterprise: FY 2018 Annual Report. https:// www.dpscs.state.md.us/publicinfo/publications/annuals.shtml*

Fries, A., Anthony, R., Jr., Cseko, A., Gaither, C. & Schulman, E. (October 2008). *The Price and Purity of Illicit Drugs: 1981-2007.* Institute for Defense Analyses.
https://www.ida.org/research-and-publications/publications/ all/t/th/the-price-and-purity-of-illicit-drugs-1981-2007

Garvey, M. (1940). *The Philosophy and Opinions of Marcus Garvey, Or, Africa for the Africans.* Majority Press.

Greene, R. (2006). *33 Strategies of War.* Viking Publishing.

History.Com Editors. (original February 28,2018, updated August 19, 2020). Jim Crow Laws. Access date. October 28, 2020
https://www.history.com/topics/early-20th-century-us/jim-crow-laws

Mander, J. (1977). *Four Arguments for the Elimination of Television.* William Morrow Paperbacks.

Samuel Stebbins. (October 1, 2019). *Special Report: America's Richest and Poorest States.* 24/7 Wall Street. https://247wallst.com/special-report/2019/10/01/ americas-richest-and-poorest-states-8/

Prison Policy Initiatives. (2018). Publications. *Maryland Profile.* State Profiles.
https://www.prisonpolicy.org/profiles/ MD.html#:~:text=Maryland%20has%20an%20incarceration %20rate,than%20many%20wealthy%20democracies%20do

Vera Institute of Justice. (n.d.)*The Price of Prisons.*

https://www.vera.org/publications/price-of-prisons-2015-state-spending-trends/price-of-prisons-2015-state-spending-trends/priceprisons-2015-state-spending-trends-introduction

Wendy Sawyer. (April 10,2017). *How Much Do Incarcerated People Earn in Each State?* Prison Policy Initiatives. https://www.prisonpolicy.org/blog/2017/04/10/wages/

Suggested Readings

Akbar, N. (1999). *Know Thy Self*. Mind Productions & Associates.

Akbar, N. (1996). *Breaking the Chains of Psychological Slavery*. Mind Productions & Associates.

Alexander, M. (2010). *The New Jim Crow: Mass Incarceration in the Age of Colorblindness*. The New Press Inc.

Asante, M. (1990). *Afrocentricity: The Theory of Social Change*. Afro World Press.

Baldwin, J. (1963). *The Fire Next Time*. Knopf Doubleday Publishing Group.

Baldwin, J. (1955). *Notes of a Native Son*. Beacon Press.

Biko, S. (1984). I *Write What I Like*. University of Chicago Press.

Browder, A. (1996). *From the Browder File Vol II: Survival Strategies for Africans in America: 13 Steps to Freedom*. Institute of Karmic Guidance.

Brown, E. (2002). *The Condemnation of Little B*. Beacon Press.

Clarke, J. (1992). *Christopher Columbus and the Afrikan Holocaust: Slavery and the Rise of European Capitalism*. EWorld Incorporated.

Davis, A. (1999). *The Prison Industrial Complex*. A.K. Press.

Diop, C. (1987). *Precolonial Black Africa: A Comparative Study of the Political and Social Systems of Euro*. Lawrence Hill Books.

Fanon, F. (1952). *Black Skin, White Masks*. Grove Press.

Fanon, F. (1961). *The Wretched of the Earth*. Grove Press.

Greenlee, S. (1989). *The Spook who Sat by the Door*. Wayne State University Press.

Jackson, G. (1972). *Blood in My Eye*. Black Classic Press.

James, G. (1992). *Stolen Legacy: Greek Philosophy Was the Offspring of the Egyptian Mystery System*. Africa World Press.

Kenyatta, J. (1962). *Facing Mount Kenya*. Knopf Doubleday Publishing Group.

Karenga, M. (2003). *Maat, The Moral Ideal in Ancient Egypt: A Study in Classical African Ethics*. Taylor & Francis.

Kunjufu, J. (1985). *Countering the Conspiracy to Destroy Black Boys: Vol I*. African American Images.

Kunjufu, J. (1986). Countering the Conspiracy to Destroy Black Boys: Vol II. African American Images.

Kunjufu, J. (1990). Countering the Conspiracy to Destroy Black Boys: Vol III. African American Images.

Martin, T. (1984). Pan-African Connection: *From Slavery to Garvey to Slavery and Beyond*. The Majority Press.

Newton, H. (1973). *Revolutionary Suicide*. Penguin Classics.

Sertima, I (1976). *The Came Before Columbus*: The African Presence in Ancient America. Random House Trade Paperbacks.

Shakur, A. (2001). *Assata: An Autobiography*. Lawrence Hill Books.

Ture, K. & Hamilton, C. (1992). *Black Power: Politics of Liberation in America*. Vintage Publishing.
Seale. B (1970). *Seize the Time.* Penguin Random House LLC.

Welsing, F. (1991). *The Isis Papers: The Keys to the Colors*. Third World Pres.

West, C. (1993). *Race Matters*. Vintage Books.

Williams, C. (1992). *The Destruction of Black Civilization: Great Issues of a Race from 4500 B.C. to 2000 A.D.* Third World Press.

Wilson, A. (1998). *Blueprint for Black Power: A Moral, Political, and*

Economic Imperative for the Twenty-First Century. African World Press.

Wright, B. (1985). Psychopathic Racial Personality and Other Essays. Third World Press.

Vanzant, I. (1996). *The Spirit of a Man: A Vision of Transformation for Black Men and the Women Who Love Them.* Harper One.